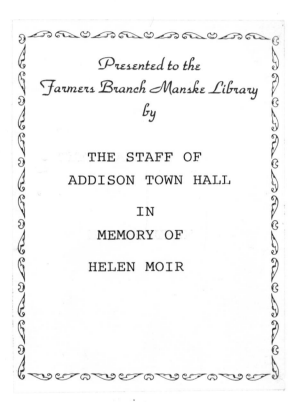

Presented to the
Farmers Branch Manske Library
by

THE STAFF OF
ADDISON TOWN HALL

IN
MEMORY OF

HELEN MOIR

...LES

Underlining in this book
present @ Checkout. CL
02-06-98

Ancestral Castles

of

Scotland

HUGH CANTLIE

Photography by
SAMPSON LLOYD

COLLINS & BROWN

HALF-TITLE PAGE: *The Old House of Cassilis*

FRONTISPIECE: *Foulis Castle*

First published in Great Britain in 1992
by Collins & Brown Limited
Mercury House
195 Knightsbridge
London SW7 1RE

Copyright © Collins & Brown 1992

Text copyright © Hugh Cantlie 1992

Illustrations copyright © Sampson Lloyd 1992
with the exception of page 1 © *Antiquaries of Scotland*, page 86 © Royal Commission on
Ancient and Historical Monuments, Scotland.

British Library Cataloguing-in-Publication Data.
A catalogue record for this book
is available from the British Library

ISBN 1 85585 0168 (hardback edition)
ISBN 1 85585 1180 (paperback edition)

Conceived, edited and designed by Collins & Brown Limited
Editorial Director: **Gabrielle Townsend**
Editor: **Colin Ziegler**
Art Director: **Roger Bristow**
Designed by: **Ruth Hope**
Map by: **Andrew Farmer**
Filmset by Servis Filmsetting Ltd, Manchester
Reproduction by J. Film Singapore
Printed and bound in Hong Kong

CONTENTS

·$\mathcal{I}$NTRODUCTION·

SCOTLAND'S PAST HAS BEEN a violent one. From the first raids by the Norwegians in 800, through to the final defeat of the Jacobites at Culloden in 1746, the Scots seem to have been fighting, whether against the English or simply each other. Throughout this time the castle has been a symbol—a visible sign of its owner's power and control.

At the start of the feudal age castles were required as places of strength and refuge. They were strategically positioned on high ground or on a promontory. Comfort was secondary, defence paramount. As the centuries passed the structure of castles naturally evolved. Advances in weaponry had to be counteracted, while greater prosperity led to expectations of greater opulence. Eventually the advent of more peaceful times and the inability of the castle to compete with cannons, changed the balance. The castles of the past became family homes where defence was not just secondary but irrelevant.

THE RUINS OF ARDVRECK CASTLE *(left). Romantically situated on the banks of Loch Assynt, in a remote part of Sutherland, Castle Ardvreck must once have been a formidable stronghold. Now it merely bears witness to how the ravages of time have destroyed ancestral castles abandoned by their owners.*

ARDVRECK CASTLE—THE HOME OF THE MACLEODS *(left). It was to this castle that the Marquess of Montrose was brought as a prisoner after his defeat at Carbisdale in 1650. He had been betrayed by MacLeod of Assynt, but at dinner MacLeod's mother refused to sit next to the chief officer of Montrose's captors. Instead she insisted that Montrose be untied and placed on her right-hand side, as a mark of respect for his loyalty to the King and his great achievements on the field of battle.*

The early period of castle building was in the twelfth century when Anglo-Norman families from England were invited by the Scottish kings to take over many of the estates. These families built their strongholds in the same manner as they had done in England, first creating a motte—a steep, flat-topped mound surrounded by a ditch or moat—and then constructing a residence of wood and clay upon it. Few, of over 250 such structures, were rebuilt in stone, so the majority can now only be traced by the massive earth mounds of the original motte.

In the thirteenth century Scotland's general prosperity led to the construction of some of its most impressive and finely-built stone castles. These took the form of massive curtain walls, some of which had a keep—for the use of the Laird and his family—inside and protective drum towers at strategic points along the wall.

This period came to an end with the Wars of Independence in 1296, when castles such as Wemyss were stormed or destroyed. The era of prosperity also ceased and such castle building that did take place over the next 70 years was either to repair damage and so make a castle defensible once more, or to provide some sort of shelter.

It was not until 1371, with the accession of Robert II, the first of the Stewart kings, that an element of stability returned to Scotland. However the country had been impoverished by the recent wars and the payment of ransoms that ensued and so castles could no longer be built on the grand scale of the previous century. A new type of castle evolved, that of the tower-house surrounded by a barmkin—a low surrounding wall—and this form was to dominate for the next two centuries. It consisted of a stone-vaulted ground floor for storage or beasts, normally reached from above by a trap door. The first floor was the principal room or Great Hall, again stone-vaulted, with an entrance doorway reachable by a wooden stair. The Great Hall was generally of double height with an intermediate floor of timber, providing the Laird with a private chamber. Above this was a lead-covered, vaulted stone roof to prevent it being set on fire by incendiary arrows.

The roof itself was the main place from which the castles were defended against enemy forces. As the techniques of defence became more advanced, the crenellated parapet was replaced by timber or stone platforms called machicolations, built out from the face of the wall,

CASTLE LEOD *(above). This is an example of an L-plan castle which was modernized at the beginning of the seventeenth century. The re-entrant was filled in to create more space for bedrooms and a scale and platt staircase, with the result that Leod took on its present square appearance.*

THE SEA GATE AT DUNVEGAN (*above*). *Dunvegan is one of the few castles whose curtain wall has survived to the present day. The Sea Gate shown above was the only means of access into the castle until as late as the eighteenth century.*

from which the besiegers could be bombarded by objects or boiling oil. Bartizans or projected turrets were built onto the corners of the keep at roof level, providing yet more overhanging defensive positions, and some of the tower houses had battered (sloped) bases, from which rocks from above would bounce off at an angle, wounding the assailants. The walls themselves were massively thick and often had mural chambers for sleeping, garderobes and cupboards built into them. Cassilis is a particularly fine example of these times, when the needs of defence dominated the castles' structural design.

The advent of gunpowder however was to revolutionize the construction of castles and, ironically, led to a decrease in the emphasis placed on defence. It was first employed by the English against the Scots as early as 1327, but it did not begin to have a decisive effect until 1460, when the use of the siege cannon became prevalent. Castle designers now began to plan their defence so as to utilize the cannon, and arrow slits gave way to gun loops. But in reality few castles could successfully withstand a sustained onslaught by cannon and gunfire and so architects mainly attempted simply to provide protection against unwanted visitors. Also, with the advent of more peaceful times, the nobility began to place less importance on defence and more on comfort.

Some of the old plain tower-houses were enlarged by the addition of a wing, so forming an L-plan,—as at Ardblair—which considerably increased the degree of comfort and privacy enjoyed by the Laird and his family. In many cases, as at Cortachy, Pitcaple and Kelburn, two wings or towers were added to the original keep, creating a Z-plan shape, which provided extra comfort and, at the same time, better defence. Sometimes another turnpike stair was added—as at Ballindalloch—or incorporated into the corner of the L-plan with a door underneath—as at Glamis.

With Flodden still fresh in the memory the Scots Parliament passed an Act in 1535 ordering the Border families to build towers of fortification which could withstand the next, inevitable onslaught from the English. Bemersyde dates from this time and, like so many other Border castles, was badly damaged during the 'Rough Wooing' in 1544–5, when Henry VIII tried to force Mary Queen of Scots to marry his son and laid waste to the south. However due to the straitened circumstances of the nobility, there was little building outside the Borders (with the notable exception of Delgatie) until the Reformation in 1560, when the Protestant nobles acquired Catholic Church holdings.

Although the threat of attack now seemed greatly diminished, there was a marked reluctance to do away entirely with some form of defence. Indeed there was a tendency to construct more modern buildings within the curtilage of the old defensive structures. Such caution proved justified at a later date, during the troubled times of the Civil War, the Glorious Revolution and the Jacobite Risings. However, in the main, the seventeenth century marked the end of castles being built to safeguard the lives of their owners.

In 1603 James VI travelled south to London with a large Scottish retinue and his courtiers were able to see for themselves the comfort enjoyed by their English counterparts and the latest architectural designs. In comparison their own castles seemed small and cramped and although there was a final flourish of castle design based on the old tower house concept, it had become outdated. Such castles as Drumlanrig, with its towers at each corner, owed much to the castles of old, but the role they fulfilled was already more one of a country house. Drumlanrig also demonstrates the Renaissance influence, which had first reached Scotland in the sixteenth century with the rebuilding of royal palaces and continued long after it was of fashion elsewhere.

Even if the building of castles largely came to a halt, this did not mean that they did not continue to be repaired when they were damaged and generally altered and enlarged in accordance with the style of the times. In the following centuries architects like Sir William Bruce, James Smith and the Adam family modernized many castles, such as the transformation of Thirlestane into a palace in the 1680s and the creation of Blair's splendid Georgian interior. Foulis, on the other hand, was destroyed in the 1745 Rising and had to be completely rebuilt.

Later still, after the State visit of George IV in 1822, some Lairds, such as those at Caprington and Pitcaple, altered their castles to fit in with the vernacular Scottish style. Then, the arrival of Queen Victoria at Balmoral stimulated another spate of building, with additions and alterations being made to a number of castles such as Blair and Murthly, by David Bryce and James Gillespie Graham.

CAWDOR CASTLE (above). The main tower of Cawdor has survived intact since it was originally constructed in 1460. It is still lived in by the Thane of Cawdor's descendants.

THE GARDENS AT DRUMMOND CASTLE (above). These ornamental gardens, laid out in 1630 with the sundial as the centrepiece, are an example of how Scottish castles were adapted to suit the changing needs and desires of their owners. As defensive requirements lessened, style and comfort became all important.

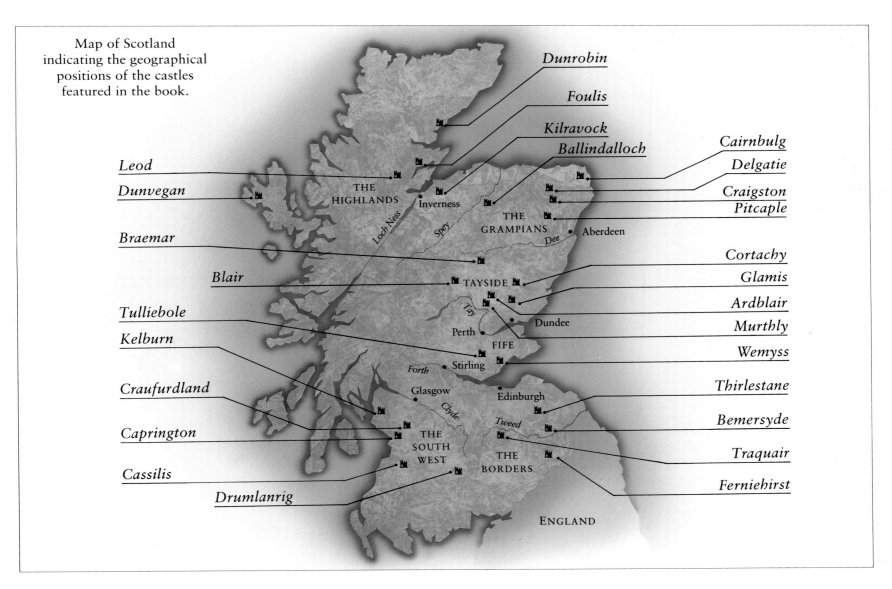

Map of Scotland
indicating the geographical
positions of the castles
featured in the book.

Dunrobin

Foulis

Kilravock

Ballindalloch

Cairnbulg

Delgatie

Craigston

Pitcaple

Leod

Dunvegan

THE
HIGHLANDS

Inverness

THE
GRAMPIANS

Aberdeen

Loch Ness

Spey

Dee

Braemar

Cortachy

Glamis

Blair

TAYSIDE

Ardblair

Tulliebole

Tay

Perth

Dundee

Murthly

Kelburn

FIFE

Wemyss

Forth

Stirling

Craufurdland

Glasgow

Edinburgh

Thirlestane

Clyde

Tweed

Bemersyde

Caprington

THE
SOUTH
WEST

THE
BORDERS

Traquair

Cassilis

Ferniehirst

Drumlanrig

ENGLAND

$\mathcal{D}$UNROBIN

T HE CASTLE OF DUNROBIN holds the dual honour of being both one of the oldest continuously inhabited Scottish castles and the home of the Earls of Sutherland, reputedly the longest established Earls of all Scotland. The origins of the family can be traced back to Freskin, a Flemish immigrant who was granted lands by David I in Duffus and Moray at the beginning of the twelfth century. However it was not until 1235, by which time the family had also come into the possession of lands in Sutherland, that Freskin's descendant, Robert, was created Earl of Sutherland by Alexander II.

Some forty years later Robert built the tower (reconstructed in 1401) which, to this day, has remained the core of the Sutherlands' family home. During the intervening centuries the family has been at the forefront of the turbulent events which have so characterized Scottish history and, like so many others, it has frequently switched allegiances from one side to another so as to ensure its own survival.

Robert's son, the second Earl, fought alongside Robert the Bruce in the defeat of the English at Bannockburn, and in 1320 his son was one of the signatories of the famous Declaration of Arbroath. The family's close links with the seat of power were further enhanced when the second Earl's grandson married the eldest daughter of Robert the Bruce. Indeed they had a son who was recognized as the successor to the throne, although he did not live long enough to inherit his birthright.

In the succeeding generations many a Sutherland was killed in battle, but they all managed to produce a male heir until 1514, when the ninth Earl died childless. His sister Elizabeth was due to inherit the title and estates but first had to fight off the claims of an illegitimate brother. The latter's ambition had been heightened by a prophecy foretelling that 'his head should be the highest that ever was of the Sutherlands'. The prophecy was indeed fulfilled although doubtless not quite in the way he

DUNROBIN IN WINTER (left). A castle has stood here since Pictish times, making this one of the oldest inhabited sites in all Scotland. It became the home of the Earls of Sutherland in 1235 and, although it has been inherited through the female line on three occasions, each time by an heiress called Elizabeth, it has remained in the family ever since. In the past the castle was the centre of one of the largest estates in Scotland, but the majority of the land had to be sold off in 1921 to meet the family's debts.

DUNROBIN FROM THE SEA *(right)*. *From this viewpoint one can clearly distinguish between the three different stages of building which together create the castle we see today. The white section, to the extreme left, is the oldest part of the castle in the picture, dating from the end of the sixteenth century. The middle section was then constructed in 1785, when the Duchess Countess rebuilt part of Dunrobin following a fire. Finally there is the newer section (1845–50) to the right, which is the work of the famous architect Sir Charles Barry and gives Dunrobin its distinctive Victorian appearance.*

VIEW OVER THE SEA *(right)*. *Perched on a hill, with a commanding view over the sea and the Dornoch Firth beyond, Dunrobin has always been in an ideal defensive position. This part of the castle was completed in 1850 and its style reflects a strong French influence. However the old defensive characteristic of the batter—or sloped plinth—is still in evidence, even if only as a design feature. In medieval times it would have served the dual practical purpose of strengthening the base of the walls to prevent them being undermined and of deflecting missiles dropped from the battlements above in the direction of attacking troops.*

had foreseen. He was captured, executed and his head was stuck onto a pole at the top of the tower of Dunrobin to serve as an example of what happened to those who dared cross the Sutherlands.

The experiences of the eleventh Earl, known for some reason as 'Good Earl John', showed that the tactic of switching allegiances did not always meet with success. First he joined the Lords of the Congregation, a movement against the Catholic Church, and was badly wounded while fighting the French at Kinghorn. He then changed sides and transferred his support to the Catholic Earl of Huntly against Mary Queen of Scots. For his pains his estates were forfeited and although he received a pardon from James VI in 1567, his run of bad luck became terminal when he was poisoned by his uncle's wife later in the same year.

During the seventeenth and eighteenth centuries the Sutherlands chose their allies rather more wisely. The sixteenth Earl was a renowned soldier who made the clan into a force locally, and despite being married to the sister of the arch Royalist, Viscount 'Bonnie' Dundee, he supported the Glorious Revolution. He later assisted the Duke of Queensberry in achieving the Act of Union and as a reward became one of the sixteen Scottish Peers elected to the House of Lords.

· $\mathcal{K}$ILRAVOCK ·

U NIQUELY AMONG SCOTTISH CASTLES Kilravock has been known as a place of refuge from the violence which has continually surrounded it. Appropriately enough, 'Kil' is the Celtic word for church and Kilravock was built on the site of an ancient chapel in which St Columba preached in 565 A.D. The oldest building which has survived until today is the substantial stone tower which was constructed in 1460, a century and a half after the Rose family first settled in the area.

Like so many of the leading families who made this part of Scotland their home, the Roses were of Norman origin and the presence of water bougets (leather saddle bags used for carrying water in the Middle East) on their coat of arms suggests that they were active in the Crusades.

Kilravock, like the Castles of Cawdor, Ironsyde and Spynie, was designed by Cochrane, a favourite architect of James III. The five-storey tower, with eight-foot thick walls, must have seemed impressively solid in those days, but it was by no means impregnable. This the Roses found to their cost when it fell to a night assault by the Mackintoshes in 1482, who set it on fire, causing £100 worth of damage.

During the course of the first half of the sixteenth century the Rose family expanded at such a rate that the tower soon became insufficient for their needs. Thus in 1553 the tenth Laird, who himself had seventeen female dependants, added the south wing and the square stair turret. Despite having to fulfil what must have been a particularly heavy procreational schedule 'the Black Baron'—so-called because of his swarthy complexion—also found the time to be taken prisoner at the Battle of Pinkie in 1547, when the Scots lost 14,000 men in their defeat by the English under Henry VIII. He was released on the payment of his ransom by three Border lairds called Pringle, who were one of the first families to follow the Reformed Church. Their support undoubtedly influenced the growing fervency of the Black Baron's own religious beliefs and practices.

KILRAVOCK (*left*). *Today Kilravock's architectural evolution is clearly visible. The original five-storey tower (on the right) with its eight-foot-thick walls was built in about 1460. Then, a hundred years later, the 'Black Baron' added the south wing and the staircase tower joining the two blocks, while the larger windows in the drawing room and library were installed by the fifteenth Laird in the first thirty years of the eighteenth century. The doocot on the left was built on the site of an early Celtic church where, it is said, Columba preached in AD 565.*

Perhaps in part due to his own domestic position, the Black Baron developed an advanced sense of diplomacy, which was to serve him well during the turbulent years that followed. He managed the exceptional feat of being well regarded by all parties and indeed took considerable care not to ally himself with any one faction. When Mary Queen of Scots came to stay in 1562 he proved to be a considerate host and yet this did not prevent him being on good terms with the Regents Moray, Lennox and Morton after she had been deposed in 1567.

His mastery of the secret of peaceful coexistence became renowned throughout Scotland and when Mary's son, James VI, visited Kilravock in 1589, he asked the Baron how he managed to live among such violent neighbours. The Baron's reply displayed his diplomatic skill to its full: 'They are the best neighbours I could have for they make me go to God upon my knees thrice a day, when perhaps otherwise I would not have gone once.' This regimen was evidently most successful, for he lived to the age of ninety.

During the seventeenth century, the Rose family proved themselves to be staunch Covenanters and Kilravock was famous as a haven for those in need of protection during the troubled religious periods which preceded the Glorious Revolution of 1688.

The fifteenth Laird succeeded his father one year before the Revolution and led a far more politically active life than his forebears. As a member of the Scottish Parliament, he joined 82 others in voting against the union with England in 1707. However he subsequently supported the Hanoverian succession and was one of the Commissioners representing Scotland in the first Westminster—as opposed to English—Parliament.

In the first Jacobite Rising of 1715 he raised some 200 of his clan to preserve peace in the neighbourhood. He then garrisoned the castle against the Jacobites, and so turned Kilravock into an asylum once again. Later he joined forces with Lord Lovat, the Frasers and the Grants and successfully besieged Inverness, which was being held by his Jacobite son-in-law, Sir John Mackenzie of Coul.

The fifteenth Laird was also responsible for some changes to Kilravock, adding the front staircase, the Queen Anne style window in the drawing room and the library. He finally died in 1732, having been

THE SEVENTEENTH LAIRD *(above). Born in 1705, the seventeenth Laird was an advocate and a Member of Parliament. He typified the family tradition of remaining impartial during times of war and politely received both 'Bonnie Prince Charlie' and the latter's enemy, the Duke of Cumberland, in the run-up to the Battle of Culloden.*

THE GREAT HALL *(right). This is still used for its original purpose—a place to feed the many guests who visit Kilravock—and is filled with reminders of the past. The narrow window, set right back into the wall, demonstrates the degree of protection the castle offered its inhabitants, while the door below, the entrance to the dungeon, serves as a reminder of the fate of guests who did not behave themselves. The weapons on the wall include broadswords which were probably used at Culloden and the bookcase on the right originally belonged to Charles Dickens, who gave it to the maternal family of the present mistress of Kilravock, Elizabeth Rose.*

happily married on five occasions—his first four wives predeceased him—, and left four sons and five daughters.

In the 1745 Rising the Rose family reverted to the more neutral stance advocated by the Black Baron. Indeed they achieved this to such effect that in the couple of days preceding the Battle of Culloden the family played host to both 'Bonnie Prince Charlie' and the Duke of Cumberland, the commander of the Government forces. The Prince came to dinner two days before the battle and while wandering with his host, the seventeenth Laird, in the garden after dinner is reported to have said: 'How happy you must be, Mr Rose, in being thus peacefully engaged while the whole country around you is in a stir.' Mr Rose's reply is not recorded, but when the Duke arrived a day later and accused the family of having entertained the Prince, he was met with the cool retort that the Roses never refused hospitality to anyone. The Duke then answered that they had acted correctly and left for the battle.

In subsequent years the Rose family have tended more to follow the example set by the fifteenth Laird than that of the tenth or seventeenth, as many have distinguished themselves in the army. During the Napoleonic Wars a number of Roses helped defend their country with honour and indeed the colours of the Nairnshire Militia still hang in the castle today. Subsequent members of the family have fought in the Crimea, the Indian Mutiny, the Nile River Campaign and both World Wars with distinction.

Today Kilravock is full of reminders of its past history—a copy of the letter from Mary Queen of Scots written in 1562, which thanks the tenth Laird for his hospitality, the dungeon in which the Covenanters hid in the seventeenth century and broadswords from the Battle of Culloden. But for the Rose family perhaps the most potent symbol is the gooseberry bush that grows at the top of the old tower. Legend has it that as long as a gooseberry bush grows on the tower there will be a Rose at Kilravock. In October 1942, Hugh Rose, the brother of the present owner, Miss Elizabeth Rose, was killed at El Alamein and four years later their father, Colonel Hugh Rose, died as well. The gooseberry bush withered just after El Alamein and, although Elizabeth claims not to be superstitious, she has since planted another gooseberry bush to replace the old one and is glad to report that it is presently thriving.

KILRAVOCK CIRCA 1720 (above). This painting demonstrates how little Kilravock has changed outwardly over the last 270 years. The only immediately noticeable difference is the lowering of the doocot's roof—a reflection of the reduced need to keep a supply of pigeons as fresh meat for the winter months.

ROBERT BURNS' TREE *(right)*. *It is thought that this was the tree under which Robert Burns composed a poem when he came to stay in 1787. His letter of thanks survives, but which of his poems he composed under the tree's heart-shaped boughs remains a mystery.*

· ℒEOD ·

ALTHOUGH CASTLE LEOD IS NAMED after a MacLeod, it has, ever since it was first constructed in 1600, been the home of the Mackenzie clan, later to become the Earls of Cromartie. They are a clan who from small beginnings gradually increased their influence until they became the second largest in the Western Highlands.

The first Mackenzie to live at Leod was Sir Roderick Mackenzie of Tarbat, the second son of Colin, the eleventh chief of Kintail. Rory, as he was more commonly known, made the audacious move of marrying into the MacLeod clan, with whom his family had a long running feud. It had all started when Rory MacLeod, the chief of the MacLeods of Lewis, had divorced his wife, a Mackenzie of Kintail, for adultery. He also disinherited his son Torquil and it was the latter's daughter whom Rory Mackenzie married.

In the end it turned out to be a fortuitous move, as, after all the various infighting in the MacLeod family had been resolved, Margaret MacLeod (Sir Rory's wife) ended up inheriting the Charters of the MacLeod land on Lewis in 1616. Making the most of this windfall Sir Rory completed the building of the castle and, perhaps in recognition of their financial contribution, incorporated the MacLeod coat of arms into his own and named his new home Castle Leod.

Sir Rory's son John was made a baronet of Nova Scotia in 1628 and his son, Sir George, was to become the first Earl of Cromartie. The latter had a distinguished if rather chequered political career. Having sided with Charles II in 1650 he was forced to flee abroad, only to return at the Restoration and become a Lord of Session. However he made the costly mistake of opposing the all-powerful Duke of Lauderdale, then Secretary of State for Scotland, and was deprived of any public employment until Lauderdale's retirement in 1677.

In 1692 he was made Clerk Register, but this proved short-lived, as he was paid off four years later when it was rumoured that he had been doctoring the minutes. However he returned to favour upon Queen

THE FRONT DOOR *(above)* AND CASTLE LEOD *(left). Above the sturdy door is the marriage stone of Sir Rory Mackenzie and Margaret MacLeod. It is dated 1616, the year that Torquil MacLeod died and left his estates in Lewis to his daughter. First built in 1605, the L-plan castle was then modernized by Sir Rory. The expense of the alterations was met by his wife's recent inheritance, which doubtless explains the origins of the castle's name.*

THE GUNLOOP *(left). The gunloop, arrow slit and bell serve as reminders of the demands of defence—even for a castle built at the beginning of the seventeenth century. By this time the arrow slit would have been largely obselete, but was still useful as a source of light. The gunloop beneath was designed to allow the defender to swivel his gun or Harguebus, giving him a wider field of fire, while the old ship's bell was doubtless used to raise the alarm or to summon help.*

Anne's succession and was appointed one of the Principal Secretaries of State. On becoming Lord Chief Justice in 1704 he was created Earl of Cromartie and he finally retired in 1710 at the age of eighty.

His grandson George, the third Earl of Cromartie, played an active part in the 1745 Rising. With his son John he raised a force of 400 Mackenzies in support of 'Bonnie Prince Charlie'. But both he and his son were captured and he was sent south for trial, where he was sentenced to death and had his title and estates forfeited.

He wrote a petition to the King for mercy, and on the Sunday after his sentence, his wife Isobel, dressed in deep mourning, took it to Kensington Palace. When the King passed her on his way to the chapel she fell on her knees in front of him and fainted. He raised her up, took the petition and granted a respite, during which time the Earl was freed from the Tower.

George was pardoned in 1749, but was not allowed to return to Scotland. Instead he, his wife and their seven daughters lived in poverty in Devonshire, before he eventually died in London in 1766.

His son John had also received a pardon and taken the opportunity to flee to Sweden. There he became an officer in the Swedish army—rising

THE STAIRWAY (*right*). *A mural staircase in the thickness of the wall was an alternative to the more common turnpike stair and it is possible that the small windows are simply arrow slits that were enlarged when the desire for light overcame the need for security.*
The statuette in the window is said to be of St George, but it is sufficiently androgynous that it could be of Joan of Arc, half of whose army was made up of Scots.

THE DINING ROOM (*left*). *Leod's old dining room is still in use today and to the right is a portrait of one of its former occupiers, John Mackenzie. He had been 'out' in 1745 and, although convicted of treason, was later pardoned. He went abroad and, having been lent the money to buy his uniform by the 'Old Pretender', enlisted in the Swedish Army. On his return to London in 1777 he was asked to raise a marching regiment of Highlanders for service in the American War of Independence and as a reward was styled Lord MacLeod, by George III. This caused much confusion among the War Office clerks who were never sure whether he was Lord MacLeod or Mr Mackenzie—a peer or a gentleman.*

to the rank of Lieutenant General—and the Swedish King conferred on him the title of Count Cromartie.

On his return to London in 1777 he raised two infantry battalions for George III and then went to India to command a battalion under Sir Hector Munro. In 1784 his estate was restored to him on the payment of £19,000 and on his death, a cousin, Kenneth Mackenzie, inherited.

From him the estates passed down the female line to Anne Mackenzie, who, in 1849, married the Marquess of Stafford, later to become the third Duke of Sutherland. She was Mistress of the Robes to Queen

THE LOCK (left). Even castles which did not possess yetts were by no means easy prey to attacking forces or common marauders. This massive lock encased in the original oak door was obviously considered sufficient protection against intruders.

Victoria and, as a personal gift, the Queen restored the family title, making her Countess of Cromartie in her own right. She later divorced her husband, but not before having two sons, the second of whom, Francis, became the fifth Earl of Cromartie. Francis had no sons and so the title passed once again through the female line to Sybell, his eldest daughter and the present Earl's grandmother.

The eighth Earl of Cromartie now lives at Leod just as his ancestors always have, except for the forty-year period when the estates were forfeited to the Crown after the 1745 Rising. And now, as in the past, it remains the headquarters of the Mackenzie clan worldwide.

*C*AIRNBULG

FOLLOWING THE BATTLE OF BANNOCKBURN Alexander Fraser of Touch was knighted for his prowess on the field and it is from him that the Fraser family so long associated with Cairnbulg descends. Sir Alexander's wife was the widowed sister of Robert the Bruce, Mary, who had survived four years as a prisoner of the English, suspended in a cage from the walls of Roxburgh Castle. And it was perhaps because Sir Alexander was his brother-in-law that Robert the Bruce was particularly generous to him, giving him a re-grant of the Charter of Touch-Fraser in Stirlingshire in 1321 and, seven years later, the Thanage of Cowie. Sir Alexander repaid his kindness by being a loyal subject right up to Robert's death, finally perishing in battle against the English at Dupplin in 1332.

Philorth, or as it is now called, Cairnbulg, came into the possession of the family some forty years later. Originally the property of the Comyns, Earls of Buchan, it had been confiscated by Robert the Bruce after Bannockburn and given, along with many other properties, to the Earl of Ross. When Sir Alexander Fraser's grandson, also called Alexander, married Lady Johana, the daughter of the fifth Earl of Ross, in 1375, he received Philorth as her dowry. It is thought likely that the oblong tower was constructed around this time and when Sir Alexander's son subsequently sold off the lands of both Cowie and Durris, Philorth was established as the principal home of the Frasers.

For the next six generations the Frasers enjoyed a period of quiet prosperity. It was not to last. The year of 1569 heralded the arrival of the eighth Laird of Philorth and the start of a period in which the Fraser name was to rise to dizzy heights before drowning in a sea of debt.

Like his ancestors the eighth Laird was called Sir Alexander Fraser and his life was dominated by his dream of turning the little port of Faithlie, nearby on the coast, into the great town of Fraserburgh. To this

MARRIAGE STONE (*above*) AND CAIRNBULG CASTLE (*left*). *This marriage stone commemorates a marriage that never took place. The Master of Saltoun was due to marry Amelia Fraser, a cousin, and so inherit her father's estates. However Amelia's great uncle, Thomas Fraser, objected to the plan and forced her father to change his will in his favour. He then captured Lord Saltoun and threatened to hang him unless he called off the marriage. This he did and Amelia's coat of arms was chiselled off the marriage stone.*

41

end he sacrificed not only his family's considerable wealth, but also his ancestral home. Immediately upon his succession he started pouring money into Faithlie. In 1671 he paid for a church and began creating a town with forty-foot-wide streets, adorned with grandiose public buildings. In 1588 he received a charter declaring Faithlie a freeport and Burgh of Barony, and another in 1592 which gave Alexander permission to build a university and make the town into a Burgh of Regality with the new name of Fraser's Burgh.

On the surface everything seemed to be going smoothly. Alexander found favour with James VI, especially when he lent him money to help him out over a few financial problems, and in 1594 he received a knighthood. However the enormous cost of the enterprise gradually consumed all he possessed and his estates, whose management he had handed over to trustees, were sold off one by one to pay for his ever spiralling debts. Eventually he was even forced to sell Philorth to some Fraser cousins (who renamed it Cairnbulg) and then he settled what little was left on his grandson in 1620, before he himself died in 1623 at the age of 86.

Cairnbulg and Frasers then temporarily parted company, though this was not for lack of effort on the part of the tenth Laird of Philorth, Alexander's grandson and namesake. Having cheated death in the Civil War, he attempted to re-establish his legal claim to Cairnbulg against his Fraser kinsman, but after many years he eventually admitted defeat and contented himself with building a house a mile away at Philorth in 1661. Nine years later he inherited the title of tenth Lord Saltoun and took his seat in the Scottish Parliament. However with the title, there also came a mass of financial problems which were to bedevil him right up to his death in 1693.

Over the following centuries Cairnbulg continued to be inhabited, but fell into an ever increasing state of disrepair. At the end of the nineteenth century it belonged to Sir John Duthie, a shipbuilder from Aberdeen, who repaired and rebuilt it. Finally, in 1934, Lord Saltoun, whose own home, Philorth House, had burnt down in 1915, bought Cairnbulg back. Flora, the twentieth Lady Saltoun, moved into Cairnbulg in 1966 and has since made it into a comfortable home for her husband, Captain Alexander Ramsay of Mar, and her family.

THE WELL (above). Not surprisingly the need for a supply of fresh water has always been a vital factor in deciding where a castle should be built. In Cairnbulg's case, the discovery of this source must have been particularly important as the location was once surrounded by coastal marshes, which made most of the water brackish.

THE TOWER *(right). Built on the foundations of an earlier Comyn stronghold in around 1375, the rectangular tower formed part of the dowry of the Earl of Ross's daughter when she married Sir Alexander Fraser. As can be seen from the sparsity of windows, it was designed with defence in mind and, although it has seen many changes, its sheer strength and size have ensured that it has survived to this day.*

On the ground floor are the vaults, which are connected to the great hall above by a trap door. Then, above the great hall is what would have been the Laird's bedroom, which is connected by a turnpike stair to another smaller room built into the thickness of the wall.

Today the tower houses the guest bedrooms, whilst the great hall acts as the family sitting room.

CRAIGSTON

ACCORDING TO THE GENEALOGY of 'The Great' Sir Thomas Urquhart, the origins of the Urquharts can be traced all the way back to Adam and Eve. This fantastical claim is rather in keeping with a family who have often shown a fondness for the romantic and strange. Sir Thomas himself translated Rabelais in the seventeenth century; Captain John Urquhart enlarged the family fortune during the next century through privateering and, preceding them both, was the 'Tutor of Cromarty', John Urquhart, who built one of the most idiosyncratic castles in all Scotland—Craigston.

Even if one discards Sir Thomas's rather far-fetched claims, the branch of the Urquhart family that built and still own Craigston can nevertheless be traced back to Adam Urquhart, who was the Sheriff of Cromarty in 1357. The Tutor was his direct descendant, six generations on, and he earned his nickname through being preceptor to his great-nephew, Thomas, who had inherited the main family estates of Cromarty on the Black Isle. It is not known when the Tutor inherited Craigston, but it must have been before 1597 as in that year a Charter under the Great Seal granted the lands and Barony of Craigfintray (as Craigston was then known) to 'Johanni Urquhart, tutori di Cromarty et Johannae Abernethy, ejus spousae'.

His plans to build a castle were delayed until 1603, when his great-nephew Thomas finally came of age, but he then made up for lost time as Craigston was built in three years, nine months—a remarkable achievement for a building of that size.

In the details of its design Craigston is quite unique, which suggests that it was built to suit the Tutor's individual taste. Its general shape, a rectangular tower with two square jambs advanced on either side, is reminiscent of the great mid-fifteenth-century Castle of Borthwick. Yet unlike Borthwick the two jambs are joined by an arch, which gives Craigston the appearance of a great square tower, even a keep. To enhance this emphasis on square strength the corner turrets were

CRAIGSTON *(left). Set in sumptuous parkland landscaped by William Adam, Craigston is one of the most idiosyncratic castles in all Scotland. It was built in the first decade of the seventeenth century by the 'Tutor of Cromarty', John Urquhart, and is most remarkable for its imposingly solid appearance. This impression of strength is enhanced by the way in which the massive, red stone quoins, quarried from nearby Turiff, have been left exposed, so emphasising the castle's square shape.*

THE DRAWING ROOM *(left). This room was remodelled by the 'Pirate', Captain John Urquhart, in the mid-eighteenth century, when he was in the process of renovating the whole castle. Amazingly the renovations took more than twice as long as it had taken the Tutor to construct Craigston in the first place—a delay which provoked the following comment from the Pirate to his son on the subject of architects: 'I also recommend you to be cautious in Entering into Buildings or Repairs of Houses: Architects and Drawers of Plans mislead Gentlemen either by their real Ignorance or designed miscalculations of the expense, which always comes out greater than expected.'*

squares instead of the more usual rounds and the upper works, apart from the balcony front with its quaint figures and faces, are less exuberant than might be expected. But the most noticeable oddity which sets Craigston apart from other castles is the massive red Turiff stone quoins which, by being left exposed, add to the overall impression of solidity and strength.

The Tutor died in 1631 at the age of 84 and he received the following rather double-edged obituary from his kinsman 'The Great' Sir Thomas: 'The Tutor of Cromarty was, all over Britain, renowned for his deep reach of natural wit, and great dexterity in aquiring (sic) of many lands, and great possessions, with all mens applause.'

Craigston was inherited by the Tutor's grandson John, as his son was considered unfit to manage the estates, having already run up debts of £40,000 Scots. As it turned out this proved immaterial as the son died immediately after attending the Tutor's funeral and indeed the grandson only survived him by three years, leaving his one-year-old son, also called John, as Laird.

John unfortunately inherited his grandfather's lack of financial acumen and in 1557, two years after he had married Lady Barbara Mackenzie, the daughter of the Earl of Seaforth, he was forced to sell the castle. In spite of receiving a knighthood from Charles II and inheriting the Cromarty estate on the death of his kinsman Sir Alexander Urquhart in 1662, his financial position deteriorated still further and eventually drove him to suicide in 1667.

The link between Craigston and the Urquharts was re-established in 1703, when Craigston was bought by Patrick Duff who later married Mary Urquhart, a great-granddaughter of the Tutor. On Patrick's death Craigston passed through his sons until the youngest, Archibald, sold it in 1739 to Mary's brother, Captain John Urquhart—otherwise known as 'The Pirate'.

He was without doubt the most colourful figure out of the historical Urquharts and thanks to a paper he wrote called 'Dangers Escaped and Blissings Received' we have a first-hand account of his many adventures. Born in 1696, he had, by the age of fourteen, already survived the bite of an otter, two near drownings, a fall from a high rock, a riding accident in a snow storm and a bad attack of measles. After a relatively incident-free

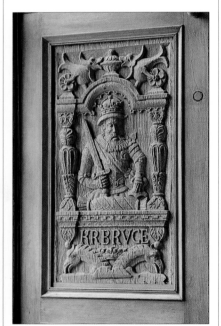

WOODEN PANEL (*above*). *When the Tutor first built Cromarty he decorated the great hall with a series of carved wooden panels. This panel, of Robert the Bruce, is one of many that the Pirate incorporated into his new drawing room in the 1750s.*

BOWL OF 'BONNIE PRINCE CHARLIE' (*above*). *This bowl was given to a kinsman of the Pirate, the Chevalier Urquhart, who had gone into exile with 'Bonnie Prince Charlie'. The Pirate himself was not 'out' in 1745, but he did however hide many fugitives from Culloden in a secret room only recently rediscovered in the thickness of the drawing room wall.*

four years he went to sea and records show that he was lucky not to have drowned on no less than three occasions. Having survived the Jacobite Rising of 1715 unscathed (he was an ardent Jacobite) he returned to sea and for a short period served with the Royal Navy in the Mediterranean under Lord Granard. But by 1723 he had transferred his loyalties to the Spaniards and had narrowly escaped being murdered by robbers in Portugal and gypsies at Cadiz. Four years later he was almost killed by a cannon ball from one of the British batteries at the siege of Gibraltar and the year of 1730 found him in America, successfully fighting off a near fatal illness.

At this time privateering was considered to be a perfectly respectable way of making a living and during the course of his various adventures John gradually amassed a considerable fortune. He indulged his passion for collecting pictures and also acquired property in the West Indies. Indeed he owned a number of plantations, one still named Craigston to this day, and these remained a profitable source of revenue for his descendants right up to the abolition of the slave trade at the beginning of the nineteenth century.

His travels largely came to an end in 1737 when he married his fifteen-year-old cousin, Jean Urquhart of Meldrum, and two years later he bought Craigston. Although he contributed financially to the Jacobite cause he did not play an active part in the 1745 Rising, instead concentrating on a number of alterations to the castle. This, in the main, consisted of adding the two wings to either side of the central block, so that by the time of his death in 1756 the exterior of the castle must have looked much as it does today.

When he died a large part of his picture collection was sold and much of the furniture was settled on his wife who went to lodge at Banff. The castle however has remained in the hands of his direct descendants to this day. It passed from father to son for three generations and then in 1847 was inherited by a daughter, Mary Urquhart, whose husband, William Pollard assumed the additional surname of Urquhart, thus ensuring the continuing link between the castle and the name.

Today it is the home of Bruce Urquhart, William and Mary's great-grandson, and he, with the help of the Historic Building Council, is still in the process of restoring Craigston to its former glory.

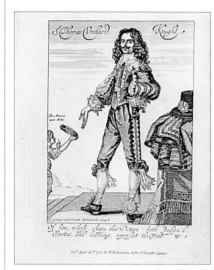

THE GREAT SIR THOMAS *(above). Sir Thomas Urquhart of Cromarty, otherwise known as the Great Sir Thomas, was a literary wit, whose most lasting contribution was his translation of the works of Rabelais. He also wrote a book on trigonometry, a series of poems and penned a number of epigrams such as: 'Take man from woman, all that she can show of her own proper, is nought else but wo.'*

THE GREAT SIR THOMAS 2 *(above). Thomas had fought as an officer under Charles I and was captured at Worcester in 1651 and sent to London as a prisoner. There he wrote a treatise in fourteen days in a vain attempt to impress Cromwell with his literary talents and so regain control of his forfeited estates. He apparently died from an inordinate fit of laughter on hearing of the Restoration of Charles II in 1660.*

THE LIBRARY *(right). The library is situated in the gallery over the front door of Craigston. It holds a remarkable collection of family papers as well as the plans and surveys of the architectural alterations made to the castle over the centuries. These archives are still being researched and have already yielded such finds as the Pirate's list of 'Dangers Escaped and Blissings Received'. This includes details of the plantations he bought in the Carribean and a manifest of the complement of slaves on Cariacou Island—so called because, according to the Pirate, it was 'Nae big enuch tae carry a coo!'*

BALLINDALLOCH

BALLINDALLOCH *(left). Originally built as a Z-plan castle, Ballindalloch has gradually been altered and extended over the centuries. Following a fire in 1645 when it was being occupied by the Marquess of Montrose, it had to be extensively rebuilt. Then, at the end of the eighteenth century, General Grant added two wings and finally, fifty years later, the castle gained its courtyard. Ballindalloch's appearance today is much as it would have been then, as later additions have recently been removed to make it a more manageable home.*

ALTHOUGH BALLINDALLOCH HAS ALWAYS occupied its present position, on the east bank of the River Avon, just before it meets the Spey, the original intention was to build the castle on higher ground further up the river. However, as fast as the builders erected a structure by day, the elements, or some other mystical force, destroyed it by night. Then one night, just when the Laird was beginning to doubt that he would ever complete the castle, he heard a voice saying, 'Build in the cow-haugh [marsh], and you will meet with no interruptions.' Realizing that a marshy site could be just as defensively effective as a cliff or a promontory, he followed the advice and the castle rose without further hindrance.

The original Z-plan format of Ballindalloch suggests that the castle was constructed in the mid-sixteenth century and this is confirmed by a fireplace in the central block, dated 1546. It is not clear if the Clan Grant were already in possession of Ballindalloch and its estate at this time, but if not, they annexed them shortly afterwards.

The Grants of Ballindalloch are descended from Patrick Grant, the twin brother of the ninth Laird of Freuchie, and during the second half of the sixteenth century they seem to have been chiefly remarkable for their feud with their kinsmen, the Grants of Casson. This resulted in a series of tit-for-tat murders spanning three generations.

Unfortunately for their tenants, the Grants' attitude towards the cheapness of life was by no means restricted to their relatives. One incident concerning a Grant Laird illustrates this graphically while also showing the extent of the Laird's authority over his clansmen. Apparently a certain Rob had somehow crossed the Laird and when it became clear that the penalty was to be death, Rob, not unsurprisingly, struck out at his captors with a marked degree of success. Indeed he was on the point of escaping when his wife, who was a witness to the scene, chided him for his lack of respect shown to his master. 'Och Rob—be quiet and dinna anger the Laird,' were her words and Rob, whose

THE WINDOW *(above). The initials above the dormer window are those of the first Baronet, Sir George Macpherson Grant. Normally such initials incorporated both those of the Laird and his wife. George, however, was unmarried at the time and, no doubt proud of his recently acquired baronetcy, inserted the letter 'S'—standing for Sir—instead.*

respect for his wife was obviously greater than that he held for his captors, readily submitted to the exhortation and went to his death without further struggle.

By the beginning of the eighteenth century the financial affairs of the Grants had run into severe difficulties, a situation which was not helped by the extravagant lifestyle of the then Laird. He was forced to place the management of Ballindalloch in the control of three of his kinsmen and when they found themselves unable to redeem the position they sold the castle and estates to a cousin, Colonel William Grant, in 1717.

In 1780 Ballindalloch was inherited by one of the most well known and colourful members of the Grant family—General James Grant. He had joined the army at the age of 22 and gone to serve in both Vienna, under General St Clair, and then the Netherlands. He travelled to America during the War of Independence and distinguished himself in both the capture of Havannah and the conquest of St Lucia, before becoming Governor of East Florida for many years. During the course of his travels he acquired a taste for gourmet food and on his return to Ballindalloch he added two new wings to the castle, one of which was to house his French chef.

Unmarried, General Grant had no known heir and so on his death in 1806 Ballindalloch was inherited by George Macpherson, a descendant of Colonel William Grant. The Macphersons were staunch Royalists and in 1745 their chief, Ewen, raised a clan company of 600 to join forces with 'Bonnie Prince Charlie'. They fought with distinction both during the retreat from Derby and the fighting at Falkirk. They unfortunately arrived too late to save the Jacobite army from defeat at Culloden, but Ewen personally rescued the Prince and hid him from the Government troops until a safe passage could be arranged to France. Ewen himself spent the next nine years hiding in a cave on his estate and although over a hundred of his tenants knew of his whereabouts, the £1000 reward for his capture was never collected.

Ewen's nephew married Grace, the daughter of Colonel William Grant and it was their nephew George who inherited Ballindalloch. In 1838 George was made a Baronet, assuming the new name of Sir George Macpherson Grant of Ballindalloch, and it is his descendant Clare who lives there today with her husband, Oliver Russell, and their family.

THE CORBEL (above). After a flood in 1829 the castle was remodelled by the Scottish architect, Thomas Mackenzie. His rebuilding was in sympathy with the existing structure and here he repeated the old style of turrets being supported by corbels.

THE COAT OF ARMS (right). Situated above the front entrance, this coat of arms combines those of both the Grants and the Macphersons. The Latin inscription at the top, Ense et animo—meaning 'with sword and spirit'—belongs to the Grants, while the lower motto—loosely interpreted to mean 'be careful how you handle me'—is that of the Macphersons. The central coat of arms incorporates the emblems of the two families—the crowns and hand-held swords of the Grants and the shields and galleons of the Macphersons.

·ℬRAEMAR·

NOW HOME TO THE ANNUAL FESTIVAL of Highland Games, Braemar's castle has in the past played host to games of a rather more bloody nature. Indeed it has been garrisoned and set fire to—once even by its owners—so often that it is a miracle it is still standing today.

When John Erskine, second Earl of Mar, first built the 'great body of a house' in 1628, he had the dual aim of providing himself with a hunting lodge for the great forests nearby and a base from which to control his tempestuous neighbours, the Farquharsons. Even if Braemar served well in its first role, it was an abysmal failure in the latter, as it has been owned by the Farquharsons since 1732.

The conflict between the two families came to a head during the Glorious Revolution of 1688. The Erskines, led by the fifth Earl of Mar, came down firmly on the side of King William, while the Farquharsons were staunch supporters of the Jacobite, 'Bonnie Dundee'. At their head was John Farquharson of Inverey, otherwise known as 'the Black Colonel', and he was not a man to be trifled with as was illustrated by his tendency to summon his servants by loosing off his pistol at the ceiling.

Braemar soon fell into the hands of the Black Colonel and the Government troops were then given specific orders to retake the castle at all costs and capture the Colonel. They successfully stormed the castle, but only arrived at Farquharson's home, Inverey House, in time to see Farquharson escaping from the back door clad in his nightshirt. The Black Colonel then gathered his men, climbed the steep rock above the castle and fired down into the enclosure. The horses stampeded and King William's crack regiment of Dragoons fled down the glen. The Colonel then set fire to Braemar to prevent it being garrisoned by Government troops in the future.

Following the defeat of the Jacobites at Killiecrankie, the Earl of Mar, who was still Braemar's owner, sent an estimated bill to King William of how much it would cost to repair the castle. But he received no

BRAEMAR *(left). Braemar is one of only two Scottish castles which were fortified as late as the mid-eighteenth century to meet the then modern standards of warfare.*
Originally built as a hunting lodge it was set on fire during the Glorious Revolution of 1688 and remained as a ruin for the next sixty years. It owes its present unique appearance—with its unusual turrets, roofline and star-shaped outer wall—to the Government, who transformed Braemar into a fortified garrison in the 1750s. In 1832 it was returned to its rightful owners, the Farquharsons of Invercauld, and became the home of the annual Braemar Highland Games. Today the sheer number of spectators has made it impossible to hold the Games at the castle itself, but it has remained the home of the Farquharson family.

reparation from the Government and the castle remained a gutted shell for the next sixty years.

The estates were finally bought in 1732, by the Black Colonel's kinsman, John Farquharson, ninth Laird of Invercauld. John had been out in the 1715 Rising under the Earl of Mar, but only after the Earl had exerted considerable pressure on him. Mar had written to his own tenants at Kildrummy from Farquharson's house, saying that if they did not join his Standard, he would send a party to burn 'what they shall miss taking from them' as an example. He also wrote that he expected the gentlemen 'in their best accoutrements on horseback, and no excuse to be accepted of'.

John wisely took the hint and duly paraded at Braemar to witness the raising of the Royal Standard, the top of which promptly fell off—much to the dismay of the onlookers, who prophesied that there would be no good from the venture.

No good did come of it and a large contingent of Farquharsons were defeated at Preston. John himself was imprisoned for a year and, probably as a result, declined to join the 1745 Rising thirty years later (for which his Deeside estates were decimated by the Jacobites). However two battalions of Farquharsons fought at Culloden under the command of a cousin, Francis Farquharson of Minoltrie. After the defeat, he was held prisoner in London for sixteen years until the Minister of Crathie walked to London in the depths of winter to present a petition signed by his parishioners and neighbours—many of whom were staunchly Hanoverian—requesting his release.

Whilst the majority of Farquharsons were harshly dealt with for their part in the Rising, John was treated leniently. This was no doubt in part due to him agreeing to lease the ruinous shell of Braemar to the Hanoverian Government, who were intent on garrisoning the Highlands after Culloden and wanted to use Braemar as a military outpost.

Thus it was that Braemar, which had been burnt down by the Black Colonel so that it could never be a garrison again, became exactly that some sixty years later.

It also received a much needed facelift to make it fit for military occupation. Under the instructions of John Adam, the elder brother of the famous architect Robert Adam, new floors and roofs were

THE DUNGEON (*above*). *Braemar's dungeon is simply a dark hole beneath the floor, twelve feet by six. Its last inmates were probably there as late as the 1820s, when Government troops used Braemar as a base from which to counter the whisky smugglers then prevalent in the region.*

THE CURTAIN WALL (*right*). *This star-shaped curtain wall was part of the many alterations and additions made by the Government troops in the 1750s, when they fortified the gutted castle to provide protection from rebellious Highlanders. Whereas arrow slits were narrow externally for added protection, the reverse was the case for musket embrasures such as these, so as to allow the defender a greater field of fire.*

STAG'S HEAD (left). Braemar was
originally built as a hunting lodge
and the hills and forests surrounding
the castle have long been famous for
their richness of game. Today that
tradition is still maintained and
Invercauld provides some of the
finest shooting and stalking
in Scotland.

constructed, the turrets were heightened and the battlemented star-
shaped curtain wall, with its loopholes for musketry, was added around
the base. The estate meanwhile was being well looked after by the tenth
Laird, an outstanding agriculturalist and forester, who is said to have
planted over nineteen million trees by the time of his death in 1805.

The main Government garrison moved out of Braemar in 1779, but
they continued to use it in the early nineteenth century as a base to
prevent whisky smuggling, which was particularly prevalent in the area

at that time. It was finally handed back to the Farquharsons in 1832 and for the next 53 years was used as the venue for the Games of the Royal Highland Friendly Society. In 1875 the twelfth Laird moved into Braemar and it became once more a family home. His mother had been the only surviving child of the tenth Laird and although married to a Ross, she had retained the name of Farquharson.

The twelfth Laird was succeeded by 'Piccadilly Jim', so called on account of his particularly extravagant habits. To fund his luxurious lifestyle he sold off a number of the family estates including Ballochbuie Forest to Queen Victoria; but Braemar gained from his extravagances as he improved many of the amenities.

Despite Piccadilly Jim's excesses, his great-grandson, the present Laird, is still one of the largest landowners in Scotland. If one includes the mountainous land which makes up a large part of the estates, his holding is estimated to be in the region of 120,000 acres. Like his ancestor, the tenth Laird, his particular interest is forestry and he reckons to have planted well over three million trees during the course of the past forty years.

Braemar today is open to the public and stands as a monument to the contradictions and ironies of Scotland's history. First built by the Earl of Mar as a stronghold to counteract the rising power of the Farquharsons, it is now—and has been for the last 250 years—the Farquharsons' home. And, while it was originally a centre for Jacobite resistance, Braemar later became an outpost of Government authority. Indeed, having been burnt to the ground so that it could never again serve as a Government garrison it then fulfilled that purpose sixty years later when it assumed its present outward appearance.

But the most remarkable transformation it has undergone was in more recent times, when the grim military fortress was converted into a comfortable family home. This was achieved by the present Laird's late American wife, Frances, whose remarkable energy and enterprise were a byword throughout Deeside.

Captain Alwyne Farquharson, the sixteenth Laird, now divides his time between three properties: Invercauld, Braemar and Torloisk on the Isle of Mull. But wherever he is staying he remains Chief of the name of Farquharson and head of the Clan.

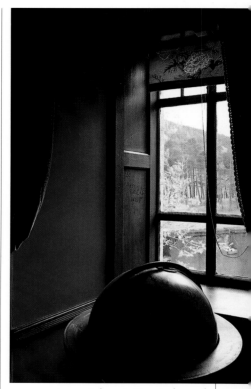

THE SHUTTERS (above). Reminders of the time when Braemar was under military occupation can still be found today. On the shutters behind the globe is the work of Corporal William Dix of Captain Lumsden's Company, XIX Regiment (The Green Howards), who carved his name there in 1757.

·𝒫ITCAPLE·

PITCAPLE CASTLE HAS, in its turbulent history, played host to royalty, acted as a prison for both Royalist and Covenant troops and, on a number of occasions, suffered terribly under the onslaught of enemy forces.

Pitcaple lies some five miles north-west of Inverurie, in the heart of Aberdeenshire and has been continually inhabited since it was built in the mid-fifteenth century. It was first the home of the Leslies until the male line died out in 1757, when, through marriage, it passed into the possession of the Lumsdens.

The land on which Pitcaple stands was given to David Leslie, the first Baron of Pitcaple and a great-grandson of Robert III, by James II in 1457, and it was David who constructed the Thane's Tower shortly afterwards. In 1511 the castle received its first royal visitor, James IV, who signed a Charter of Confirmation reinforcing the legality of James II's original gift. In 1562 his granddaughter, Mary Queen of Scots, also came to the castle and is reputed to have danced the night away beneath a large thorn bush, which survived until 1856 and has since been replaced with a tree planted by Queen Mary in 1922.

These visits undoubtedly reinforced the family's staunch support for royalty, and in 1639 they gave the Marquess of Huntly, Charles I's Lord Lieutenant, permission to use Pitcaple as his headquarters. The Leslies were to pay for their adherence to the royal cause when the Covenanters attacked and overran the castle five years later, but they did not have to wait long for their chance of revenge. Hearing that there was to be a wedding on the green in front of the castle, a band of Royalists dressed up as wedding guests and went along to the celebrations. When the garrison came out to join in the fun, the disguised Royalists edged round them, danced into the castle and pulled up the drawbridge, leaving the Covenanters on the outside.

A year later the situation was reversed once again when three Covenanting prisoners managed to lock their gaolers out of the castle

PITCAPLE AND THE FAMILY CREST *(left and above). Pitcaple was the home of the Leslies until 1757, when it passed through marriage to the Lumsdens. The latter's rather aggressive family crest used to be over the original front door. A translation of the latin motto underneath the crest shows that the Lumsdens have never been lacking in self belief: 'Thank God I am what I am'.*

and to attract the attention of some passing Covenanting troops who promptly set the castle on fire. As a result Pitcaple was extensively remodelled into the Z-plan format that it has retained to this day. The Thane's Tower was heightened and the rectangular stronghold with its stair tower was constructed on its left. At that time the castle enjoyed the additional protection of a moat, fed by an underground stream, and there would also have been a courtyard and a gatehouse. No trace of the buildings remain today, but the stream still exists, as does one of the counterweights to the drawbridge. At a later date another wing was added to the rear of the castle.

In 1650, during the space of one month, the castle played host to both Charles II and James, Marquess of Montrose, who had been Charles I's most loyal and successful Scottish commander. However the two men received a rather different welcome.

When Montrose stayed at Pitcaple it was in the capacity of prisoner rather than guest. Following the defeat of the Royalists at Carbisdale, Montrose disguised himself as a poor Highlander and for a few days escaped detection. However he was betrayed to the Covenanters by MacLeod of Assynt, a follower with whom he had sought refuge, and then escorted south as a prisoner. He arrived at Pitcaple on a Highland pony, with his feet tied together underneath, and suffered the added indignity of a herald riding in front of him shouting, 'Here comes James Graham, a traitor to his country.'

The Laird of the time was absent, but his wife, who was a cousin of Montrose, tried to help him escape. She showed him a lavatory vent which connected with a tunnel leading out of the castle. Montrose however declined the opportunity, saying: 'Rather than go down to be smothered in that hole, I will take my chance in Edinburgh.' He was also no doubt aware of the probable fate that would have befallen his cousin had his escape been successful. Ten days later he may have regretted his decision not to attempt an escape as he was hanged, drawn and quartered at Mercat Cross in Edinburgh.

Charles II's visit, a month later, was in rather happier circumstances. He landed at Garmouth and was most impressed by the countryside, saying that it reminded him of England—to this day a nearby hamlet has the name of England to commemorate the occasion. The Laird, on being

GENERAL LESLIE (above). The tenth and last Baron Leslie of Pitcaple served in both the French and Swedish armies. Earlier in his life he had run up massive debts by unsuccessfully pursuing a claim on the ownership of the nearby lands of Balquhain and, unfortunately for those who followed him, he only partially paid them off.

THE HALL (*right*). *The entrance hall in the new wing, built by the architect Sir William Burn, was remodelled in 1872 to incorporate the polished granite, Corinthian topped columns. After the Second World War the present Laird's parents further repaired and modernized the castle and in the process discovered a number of things long since built over. One such was the old well which was choked with the debris of 150 empty bottles of claret, no doubt disposed of in the past by some thirsty butler.*

told that he was expected to play host to the King that night, hurriedly bought up all the claret he could find at the local market. History does not relate whether the King enjoyed the banquet but some sort of rapport between the two was evidently established, for a year later they fought side by side at the Battle of Worcester.

The tenth and last Baron of Pitcaple was Brigadier General Sir James Leslie. During his early life he became embroiled in a legal wrangle over the ownership of the nearby property of Balquhain. In 1742, after a protracted court case, the House of Lords found against him and he was forced to pay both legal costs and three years' back rent on the estates. Crippled financially, he went abroad to pursue a military career and so missed the 1745 Rising. He enjoyed considerable success, rising to the rank of Brigadier-General in the Royal Swedish Regiment, while serving in France. But by the time he died in Lille in 1757 he had only managed to pay off a small proportion of his massive debts.

The castle and debts passed to his sister, who was married to Professor John Lumsden; and from her to her two daughters. They however found their inheritance more of a burden than a blessing and quickly handed it over to their cousin, Hary (sic) Lumsden, who was a successful lawyer. He in turn left it to his second son Hugh, and it was the latter who, in 1830, decided to transform the castle into a residence fit for a gentleman. To this purpose he hired the well-known Scottish architect Sir William Burn to design the additions, which, while being sympathetic to the old castle, were one of the first examples of the Scottish vernacular style.

Hugh's son had twelve children and in an attempt to house them all added the wing to the north of the Thane's Tower in 1872. He also further enhanced the interior by installing polished granite floors and Corinthian topped columns in the entrance hall.

Today Pitcaple is the home of Christopher and Pernille Burges-Lumsden, who have continued with the extensive repairs to the castle started by Christopher's parents. It was his mother Margaret, who, on her marriage to Captain Patrick Burges, obtained the permission of the Lord Lyon King of Arms to change the family name to Burges-Lumsden, so retaining the association of her name with Pitcaple which had first begun over 200 years earlier.

MONTROSE'S ROOM (left). It was in this room that the Marquess of Montrose was held prisoner overnight in 1650, on his way to his execution in Edinburgh. The opening in the middle was the lavatory vent down which the Laird's wife, who was a cousin of his, invited him to descend and escape. The invitation was refused so as not to bring any retribution on his cousin.

THE CHARTER OF KING JAMES II (below). This is the charter given to the Leslies of Balquhain by James II in 1457, confirming their ownership of Pitcaple. Together with all the charters and family papers from 1457 to 1742, it was discovered some years ago by the Laird's mother, at the back of a broom cupboard.

$\mathscr{D}$ELGATIE

ELGATIE IS ONE OF the foremost strongholds in Aberdeenshire and indeed lays claim to being the oldest inhabited house in Britain. Built by the Comyns, Earls of Buchan in about 1030, it came into the possession of the Hay family after the Battle of Bannockburn in 1314.

The Hay clan traces its beginnings back to 973 when the Danes invaded Scotland. Landing near Perth, they caught the Scottish army divided into two parts. While the Danes were pursuing one half of the opposing army, the fighting was spotted by a farmer and his two sons who, seizing their ox-yokes as the only handy weapons, ran down to a narrow pass and felled all who sought to pass them. Both sides assumed that it was the other half of the Scottish army and the panicking Danes turned and fled, hotly pursued by the rejuvenated Scots. Thus a potential rout was transformed into a glorious victory.

To commemorate their valour the farmer and his family were given the name of Garadh (meaning wall or palisade)—as they had stood like a wall across the pass—and their descendants became MacGaraidh. Then, when King Macbeth harried the clan in the mid-eleventh century, killing the chief and his two eldest sons, two younger sons escaped to France and translated their name from MacGaraidh to de la Haye, which has the same meaning in Norman French.

After Macbeth's death in 1057 the family returned to Scotland and were reinstated by Malcolm III. There they prospered for two centuries and a half until their fortunes took a further turn for the better following the Battle of Bannockburn. Gilbert Hay was Robert the Bruce's right-hand man at the time and together they decided that the only way to defeat the vastly superior English army was to take advantage of the Scottish weather. They therefore waited until the weather turned bad and then manoeuvred the English onto a particularly boggy patch of land in the late afternoon and kept them there all night. In the morning the bowstrings of even the most careful English archers were wet and

DELGATIE *(above and left). The main tower dates from the 1540s while its final extension, with the battlement walk above the string course, was completed in 1579. Both wings were added in 1743, with the chapel and doocot on the left (west) and the new kitchen, servants' quarters and workshops on the right (east).*

useless and the heavily armoured knights and their great horses sank defencelessly into the mud. The resulting slaughter was very great. Robert rewarded Gilbert Hay by making him Hereditary Lord High Constable of Scotland and sent him off in pursuit of the fleeing English forces. Gilbert captured and burnt two of the Earl of Buchan's castles, Slains and Delgatie, (the Earl had backed the English) and, keeping Slains for himself, set his younger brother up in Delgatie.

The basic structure of the castle we see today probably dates from this time and then it was substantially rebuilt and strengthened against artillery during the course of the sixteenth century.

There was not long to wait until its fortifications were put to the test. Following the Battle of Glenlivet in 1594, in which the Catholic Hays and Gordons defeated the Protestant forces, James VI set out to attack those who had thwarted him. He successfully blew up the Castles of Huntly and Slains but met with rather more resistance than he expected when he arrived at Delgatie. There a remarkable woman called Rohaise, a nineteen-year-old, six-foot redhead, gathered what support she could

THE CANNON *(left). This is a very light horse artillery six-pounder gun (known as a Galloper gun) which was used in the Indian Mutiny of 1857. It was brought back from India to Delgatie by the present Laird's grandfather.*

THE CANNON BALLS *(left). These three stone balls far predate the cannons which lie beside them and were designed for the twelve-inch siege guns used against Delgatie following the Battle of Glenlivet in 1594. The original intention of the besieging forces had been to destroy Delgatie completely. However, having breached the outside walls they ran out of gunpowder, which probably accounts for the unused cannon balls that remain there today.*

and put up a spirited defence for six weeks. Two siege guns had to be brought from Edinburgh by sea to Banff, whence they were dragged on slipes (sledges) to Delgatie by thirty yoke of oxen apiece.

Situated on the high ground to the west, where the Home Farm is today, they battered away relentlessly at the castle until the west wall finally collapsed. The defenders then used the escape passage to flee to the nearby Castle of Craigston and from there to France. James had almost certainly had the intention of blowing up Delgatie, as he had Huntly and Slains; but, perhaps because the siege had taken so much longer than intended, he no longer had enough gunpowder with which to do it.

The shattered west wall was rebuilt in 1597 and, unlike its predecessor, which had been between eight and fourteen feet thick, it followed James VI's dictats in not being wider than the length of an arrow and therefore indefensible against artillery.

The first shots of the Civil War were fired close by to the castle in 1639, when the Covenanters, under the command of Sir William Hay, routed the Royalists at the 'Trot of Turiff'—as the skirmish came to be known. Sir William was probably the most colourful of all the Hays of Delgatie.

He was 'bred for the wars', and like most professional soldiers was continually short of money. His father and mother—who were regarded as 'amongst the most scandalous and irregular adversaries of the truth'—tried to help him by hiding his jewellery and plate with his friends to safeguard them from confiscation. So safe were they kept, that when Sir William asked for their return, his friends refused and he had to seek legal powers to search through their Charter and other chests.

Although he had commanded the Covenanters, he was a Royalist at heart and when he changed sides in 1644, he was declared a traitor to the Government and his lands were forfeited. He then served as Chief of Staff to the Marquess of Montrose for the successful campaign in 1645, when Scotland was conquered.

Following the defeat of the Royalists at Philliphaugh he went abroad, but, with Montrose, returned in 1650, with a King's commission to raise Scotland on behalf of Charles II. They were however defeated at Carbisdale by the Earl of Argyll and then betrayed by MacLeod of Assynt. They were both tried for treason against Charles II—whom they had so loyally served—by the Earl of Argyll, and whilst Hay was beheaded, Montrose was hanged, drawn and quartered. Upon his restoration, Charles II ordered that their remains should be reburied in St Giles Cathedral and paid for the expenses out of his own pocket.

The castle's appearance altered during the course of the eighteenth century. There were a number of additions carried out in 1707 and the two wings—the chapel and Doocot to the west and kitchen and servants' quarters to the east—were constructed in 1743.

During the first part of the twentieth century Delgatie fell into disrepair and by the end of the Second World War was considered unsaveable (although it was used as a barracks for some of the 350,000 soldiers saved from Dunkirk). However in 1947 it came into the hands of Captain John Hay from his kinswoman the Countess of Erroll. He had been trained as a mason with the Bombay Sappers, and has since taken on the mammoth task of reconstruction which he is still continuing to this day.

One of the most noticeable alterations that Captain Hay has made is the newly-carved stone corbels, incorporating faces reminiscent of his time spent in the sub-continent.

GARDEN SEAT (above). *Set in an arch of the eighteenth-century, west wing addition to the castle, this seat demonstrates the changing lifestyle of the Scottish Lairds. With the threat of attack greatly diminished, they now felt free to sit outside and enjoy their gardens.*

TURNPIKE STAIR *(right). This stair is reputed to be one of the widest in Scotland—measuring over five foot. It was constructed at the same time as the original tower and is unusual for being built within the thickness of the walls.*

· CORTACHY ·

EVER SINCE THE DUKE OF ARGYLL and his force of 5000 Covenanters razed Airlie Castle in 1641, Cortachy has been the principal seat of one of the staunchest Royalist families in all Scotland, the Earls of Airlie.

The family's origins and indeed their links with Cortachy Castle can however be traced back to much earlier times. In 1163 Gilbert, a son of the Thane of Angus, was granted the lands and Barony of Ogilvie by William the Lion and from them he assumed the family name.

Cortachy was first constructed as a hunting lodge for Robert the Bruce and was acquired by Gilbert's descendant, Sir William Ogilvie of Lintrathen, in 1405. It was also around this time that the Ogilvies' close links with royalty were established by William's kinsman, Sir Walter Ogilvie. In 1425 Walter was made Lord High Treasurer of Scotland and five years later Master of the Royal Household of James I. He built up a rapport with the Stewarts which survived all the turbulent events of the coming centuries.

This great bond between the two families meant that their fortunes became ever more interlinked. At first this worked to the advantage of the Ogilvies. Walter's grandson, Sir James Ogilvie, was appointed Ambassador to Denmark in 1491 by James IV and on his return to Scotland he received the title of Lord Ogilvie of Airlie. The seventh Lord went one better when his loyalty to Charles I was rewarded with an Earldom. But all the time their nadir was approaching.

In 1641 the first Earl made the fatal mistake of travelling to England to avoid signing the Covenant against Charles I. It was during his absence that Airlie Castle was destroyed and on his return he moved into Cortachy which his family had bought back sixteen years earlier. The first Earl had his revenge for the burning of the 'bonnie house of Airlie' in 1645, when he joined Montrose and helped him lay waste to the Argyll

CORTACHY CASTLE (left). Set at the end of Glen Clova, Cortachy has been the principal seat of the Earls of Airlie since 1641. Besieged, modernized, enlarged and burnt, it was finally rebuilt as a comfortable family home in a beautifully landscaped garden and park.

estates as far as Inveraray and, closer to home, sacked Castle Campbell near Dollar, which had previously been known as the Castle of Gloom. He went on to fight with distinction in the campaigns of Montrose and played an active part in the great Royalist victory at Kilsyth, in spite of being 73 years old.

His son James fared less well the following year at Philiphaugh in the Borders. After Montrose's disastrous defeat he was taken prisoner and sentenced to death. The night before his scheduled execution his mother and sister came to visit him in his cell at St Andrews and in desperation

THE GRAVE OF DAVID, NINTH EARL OF AIRLIE *(left). David was born in Florence not far from the Palazzo San Clemente where 'Bonnie Prince Charlie' had once lived. He followed the military tradition of his family, joining the cavalry in 1876 and going to serve in India and Afghanistan. He inherited the title in 1881 upon the death of his father and continued to serve in the army, taking part in the Nile Campaign and then the Boer Wars in South Africa, where, in 1900, he was killed in action at the head of his regiment.*

he dressed in his sister's clothes and attempted a daring escape. Amazingly the ruse succeeded and he slipped away into the night, never to be caught again.

The Ogilvies were 'out' in both the 1715 and 1745 Risings. Having been attainted for high treason after the 1715 Rising, James's grandson felt disinclined to risk his life again in 1745, but his mantle was adopted most gloriously by his son David, one of 'Bonnie Prince Charlie's' most active supporters.

Although only twenty years of age, David sold the family plate and with the proceeds recruited 600 men, mostly from the ranks of his own

THE DRESSING ROOM (*right*). *It was in this room that Charles II stayed the night in 1650. He had landed at Scotland a few weeks before and been crowned at Scone at the age of twenty. He had then stayed at Perth, where he was forced to listen to six sermons a day. In desperation he had made the excuse of a hunting trip and galloped to Cortachy, where he knew he would be sympathetically received. However after staying there just one night he had to leave—as the Covenanters were close at hand—and in his hurry forgot to take his prayer book, his father's copy of Basiliki Eikon and a book on Euclid.*

kinsmen, to fight on the Jacobite side. Then he rode to Edinburgh and joined up with the Prince's army, serving at the head of the Angus Regiment. There he fought valiantly, loyally supported by his wife, with whom he had eloped from school four years earlier. At Culloden, where his wife held his spare horse, he finally realized the cause was lost and fled to France. His wife was held prisoner at Edinburgh Castle but later managed to escape and joined her beloved husband abroad.

In France, David was an instant success. Known as 'Le Bel Ecossais' on account of his charm and dashing good looks, he created his own regiment in the service of the French King and rose to the rank of Lieutenant General in the French army. His wife died in 1658, but it was still twenty years before David was permitted to return to Scotland, dressed as a Colonel in the French Guards and accompanied by a French butler and cook. He obtained a free pardon from George III in 1783 and lived quietly at Cortachy, 'much loved and respected for his charm, generosity and friendliness' until his death in 1803.

Although George III had partially forgiven the Ogilvies for their support of the Jacobites, their Earldom was not restored until 1826, when David's nephew was Laird. He was responsible for a number of additions to the castle including a new wing in Georgian Gothic style, designed by W.W. Dickson.

In 1871 the celebrated architect David Bryce was commissioned to redesign the castle in Scottish Baronial style. At the then considerable sum of £30,000, he built a spacious new wing, altered and extended Dickson's wing and added battlements and conical caps to the roofline. Inside he remodelled much of the detail and incorporated the Jacobean pendant ceiling in the drawing room, which was reproduced from Auchterhouse, another Ogilvie possession. However much of the new wing was destroyed by a fire in 1883 and after the Second World War the architect Philip Tilden was commissioned to alter Bryce's work. He redesigned the castle to suit modern requirements and, as a result, the outlines of the original castle can once again be seen to their best advantage.

Today the family tradition of loyalty to the Crown is maintained by the present Earl who has been Lord Chamberlain to Her Majesty the Queen since 1984.

THE DRAWING ROOM (right). The drawing room would have been the great hall of the original castle. Remodelled extensively by David Bryce in 1871, it incorporated a copy of the Jacobean ceiling at Auchterhouse, another Ogilvy possession. In the far corner is a little minstrels' gallery, from where entertainment was provided for the many visitors to Cortachy. Underneath the gallery is the entrance to a small circular room in the tower and off this is a door to the turnpike stair, which connected the great hall to the vaulted kitchen on the ground floor.

GLAMIS CASTLE *(left). The castle we see today is far removed from the royal hunting lodge that originally occupied the same site. Since Sir John Lyon built what is now the east wing in 1404, the castle has been added to and remodelled on numerous occasions, resulting in the impressive expanse of turrets and towers that greets the visitor today.*

THE CASTLE OF GLAMIS, home to the family of the Queen Mother, the Bowes Lyons, has a history steeped in legend. Its links with royalty go as far back as 1034, when, it is thought, Malcolm II died in a hunting lodge situated on the spot where the castle stands today. It is also claimed, in Shakespeare's *Macbeth*, that Duncan was wounded here by his cousin Macbeth; and today Duncan's Hall commemorates this most famous of the Bard's scenes.

Glamis first came into the possession of the family that was to become the Bowes Lyons when Sir John Lyons of Forteviot was made Thane of Glamis in 1372 and given the royal hunting lodge by Robert II for his services to the Crown. Sir John further enhanced his position by marrying the King's second daughter four years later and received as his reward the position of Great Chamberlain. For his coat of arms he chose a blue lion rampant—after his name—and it has remained as part of the family's coat of arms to this day. He met a violent end however, being murdered in his bed by Sir James Lindsay of Crawford in 1382, and was buried at Scone Palace on the express orders of the King.

His son, also Sir John, followed his father in marrying royalty and it was he, in about 1404, who built the first part of the castle that we can still see today, the east wing. This would, in those days, have been a narrow tower, with the kitchens in the basement and a hall above, only approachable by an outside stair.

The next in line, Patrick, continued his father's building works, creating a massive L-plan keep of two storeys. The hall was said to be so large that fireplaces were needed at both ends. Patrick also kept up his family's links with royalty. He volunteered to be a hostage for James I and on his release in 1445 was made Lord Glamis. He went on to become a Privy Councillor and Master of the Royal Household in 1450.

The family's relationship with royalty did not, however, always run so smoothly. Upon the death of John the sixth Lord Glamis in 1528, his widow Janet, née Douglas (sister of the sixth Earl of Angus), was

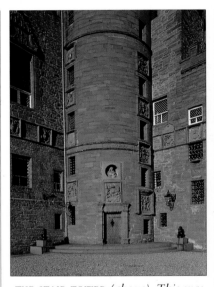

THE STAIR TOWER *(above). This was added by Patrick, the ninth Lord Glamis and the first Earl of Kinghorne, at the beginning of the seventeenth century. For the first time in the history of the castle it provided access to all floors from one front door.*

accused by James V of trying to poison him. She was tried, found guilty and burnt to death at the stake as a witch. Those accused with her did not fare much better. Her brother-in-law Forbes was beheaded; her second husband, Archibald Campbell, fell to his death from Edinburgh Castle; John Lyon was hanged and Makke, who was suspected of preparing the poison, had his ear cut off. Her son John, the future seventh Lord Glamis, was also condemned to death—the sentence was deferred until he came of age—and his estates forfeited.

Some years later their accuser, William Lyon, confessed that the charges had been trumped up, but it was not until James V died at the Battle of Solway Moss in 1542 that the seventh Lord Glamis was released

A CORNER OF THE HALL *(right). Glamis was originally built as a hunting lodge and the richness in game of the surrounding forests has provided many opportunities for Sir John Lyon's descendants to prove their prowess at the sport. This photograph also demonstrates the tremendous thickness of the outer walls, providing ample defence against any enemies.*

THE FIFTEENTH CENTURY KITCHEN *(right). This is situated underneath the original great hall, in the basement of the castle. It has been restored to the simple appearance it would have had originally.*

THE DRAWING ROOM *(right)*. *The opulence on display in this room is reminiscent of a far later period than the kitchens overleaf. It clearly demonstrates how the furnishing of the castle gradually evolved over the years, as the emphasis on defence lessened and the desire for comfort increased.*

and the castle restored to him. He soon discovered that during the time he had been in prison James V had not only built a stair between the two towers and converted the Upper Hall of the east wing to suit his own taste, but had also plundered nearly all of the castle's contents.

Despite this cavalier treatment of his grandfather, Patrick, who inherited the title at the tender age of three, became a close friend of James VI. He was made a Privy Councillor and travelled to London with James in 1603. He was created Earl of Kinghorne in 1606 for his work in preparing the terms of a Treaty of Union with Scotland—an event which did not take place for another hundred years—and it is probable that he met Shakespeare at this time, who was writing *Macbeth* for James VI.

His son John, the second Earl, fought for the Covenanters against the King and indeed spent the family fortune and more in raising an army. When he died of the plague in 1646 he had amassed debts of £400,000 Scots—large even by today's standards—for his son Patrick to pay off.

Luckily for the family Patrick proved equal to the task. He re-established the family fortunes to such an extent that by the age of forty he was able to embark on an ambitious rebuilding programme which was to continue for twenty years. He laid out a series of enclosed courts and gardens with statues in the baroque style and built a new west wing to balance the old south-east tower. The interior was completely redone although unfortunately the only work which survives today is in the chapel. He also acquired another title, so that future generations would be known as Earls of Strathmore and Kinghorne, Viscounts Lyon and Barons Glamis.

The name Bowes came into the family in 1767 when John, the ninth Earl of Strathmore and Kinghorne, married Mary Eleanor, the only child of George Bowes of Streatlam Castle and Gibside. John was running into debt and as Mary was one of the richest heiresses in England, reputedly worth over £1 million, it would be fair to presume that the match was one of convenience (at least on John's side as he was even prepared to change his name to Bowes). It was not, in any case, either a happy or convenient one as Mary made it plain that his debts were no concern of hers, and he died at sea at the age of 39 on his way to Lisbon to recover his health.

ROYAL PORTRAITS *(above). The back three photographs are of, from left to right: the Queen Mother, the Queen Mother with her husband King George VI, and the Queen Mother with the future Queen Elizabeth II. The front photograph is inscribed 'Lilibet 1935 Margaret'.*

The following year Mary married a Mr Stoney of Durham, which proved to be an even greater mistake than her first marriage had been. It soon transpired that he was also after her money, and he even went to the lengths of having her abducted by a gang of armed men in order to force her to sign over her estates to him. For his pains he ended up in prison and Mary recovered her fortune. Perhaps chastened by her various experiences she then did give her son, the tenth Earl, what she had denied his father: namely money for further repairs to Glamis.

The tenth Earl died in 1820, a day after marrying his mistress in an attempt to legitimize his son John Bowes and so disinherit his brother Thomas. In the event Thomas got Glamis and John the English estates and it was not until the latter's death in 1885 that the English estates reverted back to the family, which became the Bowes Lyons.

Any history of Glamis would be incomplete without mention of the legend of the monster who, it is said, was hidden there during the nineteenth century. According to this fictitious story, the Earl of Strathmore and his wife had a son who was so deformed that he resembled the mythical creature, the cyclops, with one eye in the middle of his forehead. They had him locked up in a small room, where he was attended to by a faithful retainer of the family, the only person outside the family let into the secret and aware of the entrance to the room.

The story goes that a house party was held at the castle while the Earl and his wife were away and, determined to prove the story right or wrong, the guests hung a towel out of every window they could find. They then assembled on the lawn below and sure enough there was one window which had no towel. The Earl however returned before they could pursue the matter any further and so it has remained in the realms of fiction.

The Queen Mother's father was the fourteenth Earl and it was at Glamis that she spent part of her childhood. Upon her marriage to the future King George VI, private apartments were set aside for their use— indeed they are the same rooms that James V occupied in the sixteenth century. The Queen Mother's nephew, Fergus, became the seventeenth Earl in 1972 and, with his wife Mary, the Countess of Strathmore, restored the private apartments of the castle. They are now occupied by their son Michael, the eighteenth Earl, and his family.

ENGRAVING OF GLAMIS CASTLE *(right). This engraving by J. Walker, from an original sketch by J. Moore, shows Glamis in a rather more derelict state at the end of the eighteenth century. The gardens, constructed so carefully by the third Earl of Strathmore and Kinghorne, have become overgrown, and even the castle appears to be crumbling away.*

·Murthly·

MURTHLY (*left*). Murthly was
originally a royal hunting lodge and
the tower was built on older
foundations in 1405. A hundred
years later another crow-stepped
gable tower was added, so forming
an L-plan castle with a turnpike
stair in the angle. It
came into the possession of the
Stewarts in 1615, who later
constructed the east and north wings
creating the courtyard seen here. The
grand, classically styled entrance
with its Venetian window was
added in 1790.

MURTHLY HAS BEEN THE PROPERTY of the Stewart family since Sir William Stewart 'the Ruthless' acquired the castle through blackmailing his Abercrombie cousin in 1615.

Sir William, whose father had been a courtier to Mary Queen of Scots, was born at Court at much the same time as the future King James VI. The two enjoyed a lifelong friendship and William took full advantage of his influential position to augment his family's fortune.

Sir William's first opportunity came in 1600 when he and the King were out hunting with a party of friends in Fife. During a break for lunch the Earl of Gowrie rode up to the King and informed him that there was a man at his house in Perth who would give James a crock of gold if he came and visited him alone. Rather naively the King consented and the hunting party rode back to Perth, where the King entered the Gowrie house. After quarter of an hour had passed and the King had still not emerged, Sir William became suspicious and demanded to see James. On being told that the King had already left from another exit, the party made ready to follow him, but at that moment precisely a small window in a garret flew open and the King was heard shouting for help. Sir William and the others immediately broke into the house, slaying all who stood in their way, and found the King locked in the garret, struggling with Gowrie's son Ruthven. Without hesitation Sir William ran Ruthven through and escorted a thoroughly dishevelled and shaken King outside to safety.

This escapade, since known as the Gowrie conspiracy, led to the King expropriating all the properties of the Gowries, and, as a reward for his help, he gave Sir William the lands of Strathbran, which bordered Sir William's own estate of Grantully.

His acquisitive appetite no doubt whetted, Sir William then set his sights on the neighbouring estate of Murthly. The fact that it belonged to his cousin Abercrombie proved to be no more than a temporary hindrance. He simply accused Abercrombie of harbouring Jesuits and

THE MARRIAGE STONE (*above*). *The
initials on the stone are those of Sir
Thomas Stewart and his wife, Dame
Grizel Menzies. He was apparently
'a knight of somewhat grim aspect,
but gorgeous in apparel'. But
however grim his apparel, his
descendants owe him a considerable
debt as it was he who built the north
and east wings and laid out the
formal gardens in 1660.*

THE GARDEN HOUSE *(left)*. *This building, with its distinctive ogee-capped roof, was sketched by Sir Robert Lorimer for one of his designs. It is one of the few additions that have been made to the gardens since it was laid out by Sir Thomas Stewart in 1660. The present Laird has been actively involved in restoring the gardens to their original state.*

threatened to say as much to James VI unless Abercrombie sold Murthly to him for a nominal sum. His cousin, having no choice, signed the necessary papers and so Murthly came into the possession of the Stewart family.

By this time Murthly was already a typical L-plan castle. The original five-storey fortified tower was probably constructed in the fifteenth century and the capped turrets and crow-stepped gable tower added in the next century.

The baronetcy came into the family in 1720, when the ownership of Murthly passed to a cousin, Sir George Stewart, whose father, an eminent lawyer, had been made a baronet in 1683. And it was through Sir George's son John that the family became embroiled in a famous scandal. John had taken, as his third wife, Lady Jane Douglas (whose grandson from an earlier marriage was later to inherit the Douglas fortune) and despite being over forty she soon became pregnant. Determined not to let her condition influence their movements the couple set off to France for a holiday when her pregnancy was already at an advanced stage. On a particularly bumpy journey to Paris the inevitable happened. The result, as far as she was concerned, was twins, one of whom later died: but the real truth only came out some years later, when the surviving twin laid claim to the Douglas Dukedom.

The claim went to court and it was only there that Sir John and the midwife admitted what had really happened. Both of Lady Jane's twins had been stillborn and to save her any anguish, Sir John had found two other newly born twins nearby that he had substituted. The result of the case was that the son not only lost his claim on the Douglas fortune but also on Murthly.

The sixth Baronet, Sir John Drummond Stewart, succeeded in 1827. Earlier in his life he had made a grand tour of Europe and acquired a vast amount of furniture and paintings. On his return he resolved to build a castle worthy of housing them and commissioned the Gothic Revival architect, James Gillespie Graham, to create 'the largest private house in Scotland'. The intention had been to pull down the old castle, but fortunately for his descendants he ran out of both time and money, dying in 1838, and the title and estates passed to his flamboyant younger brother, Sir William 'Buffalo' Stewart.

THE CHURCH *(right). This was the first church in Scotland, built after the Reformation, to be consecrated as a Catholic place of worship. Sir William 'Buffalo' Stewart commissioned the architect James Gillespie Graham and his famous pupil A.W. Pugin to construct it as an extension to the old funerary chapel.*

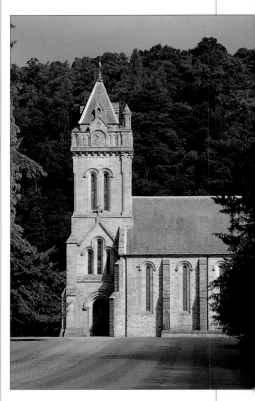

Sir William had spent much of his early life travelling, mainly in North America, where he made his money trading in furs. He returned to Scotland on his brother's death, bringing with him, among other things, various trees and shrubs indigenous to America (many of which still survive today) and a herd of buffalo which continually escaped and, on one occasion, held up the trains on the main line to Inverness.

He apparently detested his family and had vowed never to sleep under Murthly's roof. For this reason he insisted on staying in a cottage on the estate, until the east wing had been rebuilt to his taste, using material from the by now defunct new castle (it was eventually demolished in 1949). So great was his loathing of anything to do with his family that he gave his servants instructions to wake him at once should he ever fall asleep in any part of the castle that he himself had not either constructed or remodelled.

William outlived his own son and, as the title and estate were entailed, William was unable to prevent his younger brother, Sir Douglas Stewart, from inheriting. Sir Douglas's first act was to exhume his brother's body from its resting place in the church, but Sir William did at least have the last laugh as he left all the contents of Murthly to his adopted, and presumably illegitimate, Texan son, Frank Rice Nicholls. Frank proceeded to sell everything off immediately and the family have been trying to buy it all back ever since.

Douglas proved to be the last Baronet as he died childless in 1890 and the castle and estates passed to a fifth cousin thrice removed, Colonel Walter Steuart-Fothringham. This was despite Douglas having a number of closer relations and was due to an obscure entail created by Sir Thomas, the grandson of Sir William 'the Ruthless', in 1717. Sir Thomas had been an ardent Jacobite who had been fined heavily for his loyalties and, fearing that such beliefs could lead to the estate being forfeited to the Crown in the future, he drew up an entail whereby the castle could never pass to a Jacobite.

Today Murthly is the home of Robert Steuart-Fothringham who has been particularly active in restoring both the castle and chapel. Otherwise the castle remains much as it was in the time of Sir William 'Buffalo' Stewart—a mixture of styles reflecting the legacies of the different generations.

THE YEW WALK (above). This walk from the house to the church is used by the Lairds of Murthly on only one occasion—on the way to their own funerals.

THE BALLROOM (*right*). *This was rebuilt after a fire completely gutted the east wing of the castle in 1852. Lord Mansfield, who was staying at the time, was awoken by his manservant with the words: 'Arise my Lord, the castle is in flames.' His Lordship hurried down the stairs carrying a silver candlestick which has apparently never been returned. The portrait at the end is of Sir William 'Buffalo' Stewart, who commissioned the rebuilding works. It shows him as a young officer of the 17/21 Lancers at the time of Waterloo, where he fought with distinction. The picture was recently bought back by the family from an American art museum.*

·BLAIR·

BLAIR HAS BEEN THE SEAT of the Earldom of Atholl since Celtic times and the castle's position, strategically situated on the main route through the Highlands, makes it likely that some form of defended building existed there even earlier. However the first recorded reference to a castle is in 1269, after the original Celtic line had died out and the Earldom had passed through the female line to the Strathbogies. On his return from the crusades David Strathbogie, the Earl of Atholl, complained to Alexander III that while he had been away, a certain John Comyn had trespassed on his land and even had the cheek to build a tower. Since known as Cumming's Tower, it has formed the central structure of the castle to this day.

The rift between John Comyn and the Strathbogies was healed when John Comyn's granddaughter married a Strathbogie. But the two families did not have long to enjoy their new found friendship as they

BLAIR CASTLE (left). One of the most famous castles in Scotland, Blair has been the seat of the Earldom of Atholl since before the Crusades. The oldest part of the castle is the tall tower in the centre known as Cummings Tower, which was built without the landowner's permission in 1269. Since then Blair has been attacked on many an occasion and was indeed the last castle in the British Isles to be laid siege to— during the final Jacobite Rising.

THE GROUNDS (left). It was in these surroundings that the third Earl of Atholl hosted a two-day hunting party in 1529 and, to house his guests, built a luxurious village said to rival the extravagance of the Field of the Cloth of Gold created by Henry VIII for his jousting tournament in France. When his guests left, the Earl simply set the whole village on fire.

made the fatal mistake of opposing Robert the Bruce at Bannockburn. The result was that they forfeited both the title and estates to the Crown.

In 1457 the Crown granted first the estates and then the title to Sir John Stewart of Balvenie, James II's maternal half-brother. He served James III loyally, suppressing a rebellion by the Lord of the Isles in 1475. However his loyalty backfired in 1488 when he supported James III against the future James IV and was taken prisoner. He died in 1512 and when his son followed suit the next year his grandson inherited.

The third Earl was famous for his hospitality and in 1529 invited James V, the latter's mother and the Papal Nuncio to a two-day hunting

THE ATHOLL HIGHLANDERS *(left)*. *This photograph shows the Sergeants of the Atholl Highlanders in 1884. The regiment was originally formed in 1778 to fight in the American War of Independence. In 1783 they refused to obey orders to go and serve in India and although the War Office was forced to admit that they were entirely within their rights, the Regiment was eventually disbanded. However in 1839 it was reformed and fulfilled the role of bodyguard to Queen Victoria when she visited Scotland in 1844. The following year they were presented with their colours and today remain the only legal private army in Europe.*

party. As there was not enough room to house them and their retinue in the castle, he created a special village in the castle's grounds with lodges made of timber and furnished with rare tapestries and ornaments. It was said to have been on a par with the famous 'Field of Cloth of Gold' created in 1520 for Henry VIII and Francis I's jousting tournament in France. However, much to the horror of the Papal Ambassador, the Earl set fire to the village and all its valuable furniture on his guests' departure, and the next year built a great hall at Blair Castle to accommodate any future visitors.

The fifth Earl died without male issue in 1595 and so the title reverted once again to the Crown. However the Earl's daughter, Lady Dorothea

Stewart, married William Murray, the second Earl of Tullibardine and their son was subsequently awarded his grandfather's old title by Charles I in 1629. Since then the title has remained in the Murray family.

William was a staunch Royalist and although Blair was free from attack during his lifetime, it was stormed by Cromwell's troops in 1652. Unfortunately there was a magazine of gunpowder in the castle which the troops were unable to remove when they left and so they blew it up *in situ* causing considerable damage to Blair's structure. The second Murray Earl, who became a Marquess in 1676, started rebuilding the castle in 1684 and he was sufficiently advanced in his work for Blair to be a valuable stronghold for the army of James VII, under the command of Viscount Dundee, a few years later. Indeed it was from Blair that Viscount Dundee set out for Killiecrankie on that fateful day in 1689, when, despite leading his troops to a glorious victory, he lost his own life and with it all hope of Jacobite succession.

The Marquess died in 1703 and was succeeded by his son John, later to become the first Duke of Atholl. John had supported the Glorious Revolution of William and Mary and continued to back the Government during the first Jacobite Rising. However his eldest son William, Marquess of Tullibardine, and two younger sons, Charles and George, were Jacobites and so on John's death in 1724 it was the next eldest son, James, who inherited.

The divisions within the family continued in the 1745 Rising when James supported the Government and his brothers, William and George, sided with Bonnie Prince Charlie. Matters came to a head when George, as head of the Jacobite army, had the dubious distinction of laying siege to his own home. It turned out to be the last siege in the history of the British Isles and left Blair badly damaged.

Since then the castle has undergone two metamorphoses. The first, in the mid-eighteenth century, resulted in the removal of the top two storeys of Cumming's Tower, the parapets, turrets and crenellations. So complete was the transformation, that on a visit in 1844, Queen Victoria described it as 'a large, plain, white building'. Then, in line with the fashion for Neo-Scottish Baronialism, the famous Scottish architect David Bryce was commissioned to redesign it and the result is the castle we see today.

THE MAIN STAIRCASE (*above*). *Today the wall is hung with the weapons and trophies of a bygone age. The muskets would have been used during the Napoleonic Wars and probably in 1797 during the Perthshire Militia riots.*

TULLIBARDINE ROOM (*above*). *This is the room 'Bonnie Prince Charlie' occupied when he stayed at the castle in 1745. The second Duke of Atholl was not present as he was a supporter of the Government, but his elder brother, the Marquess of Tullibardine, and younger brother, Lord George Murray, were in the group of seven men who came over from France with the Prince.*

KNEELING UNICORN *(above). The stone carving of a kneeling unicorn, the heraldic beast of Scotland, and a man playing a lute lie above the coat of arms of the Blairs of Balthycock, which is positioned over the main door. Their origin is unknown.*

ARDBLAIR *(left). The castle was built on the foundations of an earlier fortress dating back to Pictish times. The tower seen here was constructed in 1540 and is the oldest part of the castle surviving today.*

THE PEACEFUL ATMOSPHERE OF ARDBLAIR, today run as a farm by its owner Laurence Blair Oliphant, stands in marked contrast to the violent past of both the area and Laurence's ancestors. Geographically, Ardblair's situation has changed radically over the years. As the Gaelic word 'ard'—meaning promontory—suggests, it was once surrounded on three sides by a loch. Then the site of a Pictish settlement, the ease with which the spot could be defended made it a site of considerable strategic importance. As the centuries passed and the loch drained away, the second part of its name—blair—assumed an added significance. Originally Blair, or blar, simply meant a plain clear of woods, but as the Celts always chose such a place for their hostile encounters, the word at length took on more sinister undertones, signifying a field of battle.

In 1399 Robert III granted the lands of Ardblair, which at the time amounted to a fifth of the entire parish of Blairgowrie, to Thomas Blair. As befitted their name and their new home, the Blairs were a warmongering family who were continually feuding with their various neighbours. Indeed there is a record of a group of Blairs being summoned for their part in the murder of Lord Drummond of Leidcrieff and his son in 1599, and while most of them managed to find an adequate alibi, one of their number, Patrick Blair of Ardblair, was convicted and beheaded.

Not surprisingly their behaviour was not received with universal acclaim by their neighbours and towards the end of the sixteenth century the Blairs built an L-plan tower so as to afford themselves better protection. This forms the north-west section of the present castle and is remarkable for incorporating one of the few left-handed turnpike stairs in Scotland.

The last of the Blairs of Ardblair was James and, on his death in the first half of the eighteenth century, Ardblair passed to his daughter Rachel, who married Dr John Robertson of Edinburgh. They in turn

HEAD OF BACCHUS *(above). This was originally at another property of the Blair Oliphants—Dalguise House. However when the house was sold to the Association of Boys Clubs after the Second World War, the Governors decided that the God of Wine was a rather inappropriate symbol for the boys and the statue was transferred to its present resting place in the courtyard at Ardblair.*

BUST OF ROBERT THE BRUCE *(above)*.
*The skull of Robert the Bruce, whose
daughter married an Oliphant, was
found in the ruins of Dunfermline
Abbey in 1819 and a cast of the skull
was made before it was reburied.
This bust, created by Lady Freda
Rollo, was based on the cast and
therefore does not have the beard
that Robert would have indubitably
sported during his life.*

failed to produce a son and their daughter Christian married Laurence
Oliphant. The couple inherited the castle in 1792 and thus two great
Scottish families, the Blairs of Ardblair and the Oliphants of Gask,
became united, not just in property but also in name, as in a
demonstration of respect for his wife's ancestry, Laurence changed his
name to Blair Oliphant.

Laurence's ancestors have an impeccable Scottish pedigree. Sir
William Oliphant defended Stirling Castle from Edward I's besieging
forces for three months in 1300 and then, after the Scots had won it back
three years later, he was again appointed Governor and it was the only
fortress to defy King Edward's power. Finally forced to surrender in July
1304 Sir William spent four years imprisoned in the Tower of London.
Later he was one of the signatories to the Declaration of Arbroath,
which included that famous sentence: 'While a hundred Scots remain
alive, we will never submit to the domination of the English.'

The reputation of the family was tarnished by the fifth Lord Oliphant
who succeeded to the title at the age of ten in 1593. His only achievement
was to dissipate the family fortunes and he even failed to provide a male
heir. He therefore resigned his title and estates in favour of his cousin
Patrick Oliphant, although the transfer was only confirmed by Charles I
much later, in 1633. Patrick's son, the seventh Lord, reverted to the ways
of his ancestors and was one of the peers who bitterly opposed the
Treaty of the Union in 1707. The title was lost with the death of his
youngest brother in 1757, as the heir, Laurence Oliphant, was not
allowed to assume the title on account of his Jacobite sympathies.

Laurence had been out in the 1715 Rising and in 1745 he was joined by
his son, also called Laurence, who was an aide de camp to 'Bonnie Prince
Charlie' and later became the seventh Laird of Gask. Together they
served the Prince throughout the campaign as officers in Strathallans
Horse. Both survived Culloden unhurt and then escaped abroad where
they lived for the next seventeen years. The younger Laurence never
renounced his Jacobite sentiments and to his death refused to allow the
names of the reigning monarch and his queen to be mentioned in his
presence, insisting that they only be referred to as 'K' and 'Q'.

It was the seventh Laird's son, also called Laurence, who married
Christian and the present Laird is their direct descendant.

THE COURTYARD *(right). Although it is not known exactly when the courtyard was created, the central arched gateway which leads into it carries the date of 1668. The hall and the south wing, which now stand in the place of the original retaining wall, date from the nineteenth and the beginning of the twentieth century respectively.*

·TULLIEBOLE·

THE HALLIDAYS, OWNERS OF TULLIBOLE from the late sixteenth century until 1722, when it passed through marriage to the Moncrieffs, are an ancient Border clan, whose name derives from the word holiday. When the clan decided on a plundering excursion across the English border, their rallying cry was 'holiday' as they viewed the activity as a break from the boring drudgery of everyday life. Indeed the small hill on which they used to assemble on such occasions has retained the name Halliday Hill to this day. When the clan first adopted the name is unknown, but by the time of the Crusades the family was large enough for a 1000 strong force of Hallidays to have served in Palestine.

Officially the Hallidays' ownership of Tullibole dates from 1598, when an Edinburgh advocate, John Halliday, bought the castle. But the fifteenth-century marriage between Theobald Halliday and Miss Hay of Tullibole suggests the family's links with Tullibole far precede this. The castle in its present form was constructed by John Halliday together with his son, Sir John and the marriage stone above the front door gives its date of completion as 1608. However the presence of a castle on this site is mentioned in the letters of Edward I dated from 1304 and it is known that James VI was in the habit of stopping off there during the annual move of his Court from Stirling to Falkland. It is therefore now thought that the west wing was originally a free-standing tower with a turnpike stair at the north-east angle and that even the eastern section may have pre-1608 work incorporated into it.

In 1722 Catherine Halliday, the daughter and heiress of John Halliday (a descendant of Sir John), married the Reverend Archibald Moncrieff, who obtained the estate of Tullibole in her right. The Moncrieffs are an old and distinguished family, who gained a charter of Barony in 1495. Three generations later Sir John Moncrieff got into such financial difficulties that he had to sell his Moncrieff estate to his cousin Sir Thomas Moncrieffe, whose successors are the Moncrieffes of that Ilk.

THE FRONT DOOR *(above). The marriage stone over the front door bears the initials of Sir John Halliday and his wife and the date of 1608. It was probably at this time that the square stair-tower was constructed, next to the existing external turnpike stair that can be seen to the right of the picture.*

Archibald's branch of the family have been by tradition men of the Church or the Judiciary (and occasionally both!). Archibald's son, although following his father into the Church, did not manage to stay on the straight and narrow financially and was forced to sell Tullibole to his wife's uncle, Henry Wellwood, in 1749. However the castle soon returned to the direct family as Henry made it over to William's two-year-old son, also called Henry, three years later. Henry, later to become the eighth Baronet, also entered the Church and, if anything, surpassed the achievements of his forebears. He was known for the devoted zeal and fidelity with which he carried out his clerical duties and in 1785 he was elected moderator of the General Assembly.

On his death in 1827 he was succeeded by his second son James, who was the first of the family to enter the Judiciary. In the year in which he became the ninth Baronet he defended the murderer Burke and his associate Hare on the grounds that despite their poverty and the instinctive horror provoked by their actions, they were still entitled to a defence counsel. Two years later he was elevated to the bench and then made Lord of Session, where he became renowned for his dispassionate weighing of evidence.

James's son, Henry, reverted to the Church and was one of the founding members of the Free Church of Scotland in 1843, while the next two generations followed James's example in becoming judges. James, the eleventh Baronet, was the presiding judge at the famous trial of the poisoner Madeleine Smith and in 1873 he inherited the original Moncrieff Baronetcy dating from 1626. His son Henry James became a judge while his father was still alive—a situation which caused considerable confusion at a reception given for Queen Victoria. His father possessing the title of Lord Moncrieff, Henry James was introduced as Lord Wellwood and his wife as Mrs Moncrieff. Queen Victoria was apparently most taken aback as she presumed they must be living together in sin and it is reportedly as a result of this encounter that the wives of judges are now styled as Ladies, so as to avoid any similar embarrassing misunderstandings.

Henry James was succeeded by his brother Robert and it is his grandson, the fifth Lord Moncrieff and fifteenth Baronet, who today lives at Tullibole with his son and daughter-in-law.

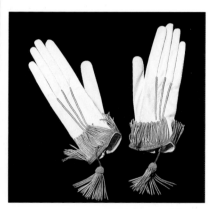

THE JUDGE'S GLOVES (above). These gloves were given to the first Lord Moncrieff in 1881, when, as Justice Clerk, he visited Dundee only to find that there were no cases to try. This was known as a Maiden Assize and on such an occasion it was the custom to present the presiding judge with a pair of white gloves.

THE GREAT HALL (*right*). *Originally this room would have possessed an intermediary timber floor where the Laird would have had his private room. Access was by a straight mural staircase built into the thickness of the wall on the left, which led to the existing but now useless door halfway up the wall. His fireplace can still also be seen as can the original window, now boarded over. When the castle was modernized in the seventeenth century the timber floor was taken out and a new window formed.*

WEMYSS CASTLE (left). The main rectangular tower was built in the fourteenth century on the site of the original castle, that had been burnt to the ground by Edward I. After the Restoration in 1670 the second Earl designed and constructed a new L-shaped wing to the west. The result is plain but imposing.

THE WEMYSS FAMILY ARE SAID to be descended from Macduff, Shakespeare's well-known Thane of Fife, and their ancestry can be traced back to the thirteenth century.

During the Wars of Independence they at first supported Edward I and indeed two of the family were sent to Norway to escort the Maid of Norway back to Scotland for her proposed marriage to Edward II. However as the war progressed they changed their allegiance to Robert the Bruce, which caused Edward I to seek revenge by sacking the castle.

The massive rectangular tower which forms the basis of the castle we see today was probably built during the fourteenth century and enlarged in the sixteenth century by Sir John Wemyss to house his royal visitors. Sir John was a great supporter of Mary Queen of Scots and it was at Wemyss that she first met her future husband, Henry Lord Darnley.

Sir John's grandson was elevated to the title of Earl of Wemyss, Elcho and Methil in 1633 and, before his death in 1649, he had been both High Commissioner to the General Assembly and a Privy Councillor. But it was his son David, the second Earl, who was finally to establish the reputation and fortunes of the family.

In marked contrast to many of his peers he took an active interest in his estate. When coal was discovered on his land he not only set about mining it but built a harbour nearby at Methil to ship it to England, Holland and the Baltic. He further enhanced his entrepreneurial reputation by taking advantage of the high price that salt fetched at the time. He evolved a system whereby sea water could be evaporated in shallow pans over a fire fuelled by the plentiful supply of coal.

He did not become directly involved in Scotland's politics, but did play host to Charles II in 1650, shortly after the latter had been proclaimed King, and again just before the disastrous Battle of Worcester, which resulted in the occupation of Scotland by Cromwell. After the Restoration in 1660 and the return of more settled times, he embarked on a comprehensive building programme to create more

THE INNER COURTYARD *(above). Originally the courtyard was much bigger than it is today. During the sixteenth century additional buildings were fitted in, to house the growing family and many visiting guests, such as Mary Queen of Scots.*

space for his three successive wives and seventeen children. Despite only
two daughters surviving childhood, the youngest had the decency to
marry her cousin, Sir James Wemyss, and so keep the title in the family.

The third and fourth Earls further enhanced the family fortunes by
marrying the eldest daughter of the Duke of Queensberry of Drumlanrig
and the daughter of the wealthy Charteris of Amisfield respectively.

David, the fourth Earl, was an ardent Jacobite and following the
defeat of the Jacobites at Culloden in 1746 was forced to flee to
Switzerland, where he died in 1787. This led to the break-up of the
Wemyss title and estates with his next brother, Francis, assuming the
title and the Charteris estates, and his youngest brother, James, the
estates and Castle of Wemyss.

James's grandson married Millicent, the forceful granddaughter of
William IV, and on her husband's death in 1864 she took over the
running of the estate with considerable success for the next thirty years.
Today Wemyss Castle is the home of Captain David Wemyss who lives
there with his mother, the indefatigable Lady Victoria Wemyss. Now
over a hundred years old she provides not only a direct link to William
IV, but is also the last surviving goddaughter of Queen Victoria.

Thirlestane

A SIDE VIEW OF THIRLESTANE (left). The original keep was completed in 1590 and since then has been added to on two separate occasions. The first was in the 1670s when the second Earl (later Duke) of Lauderdale employed the architect Sir William Bruce to give the castle a more palatial feel. The latter was responsible for the addition of the two front towers and the front staircase which together dominate the approach to the castle. Then, in the 1840s, two Victorian wings, designed by David Bryce and William Burn were built. As can be seen in the photograph, the stonework of the Victorian wings (one is to the right) is noticeably darker than the creamy colour of the central keep.

THIRLESTANE CASTLE IS THE HOME of the Maitlands, the family of one of the most powerful figures in Scotland's history, the Duke of Lauderdale. The family came to England with William the Conqueror in 1066 and first settled in Northumberland.

Originally Thirlestane was the site of a fortress built by Edward I at the end of the thirteenth century. However the present castle dates from the late sixteenth century when the estates of Thirlestane were inherited by John Maitland. He had been made Lord Chancellor of Scotland and created first Lord Thirlestane as a reward for his steadfast support of James VI. John then decided to build a home in keeping with his new position and the result, constructed around 1590, was the basis of the castle we see today; a long, narrow keep, with towers at each corner and three small towers on each side.

The Lord Chancellor, although an undoubtedly successful and influential figure was but a pale shadow of his grandson, the second Earl and only Duke of Lauderdale. Also called John, he was born in 1616 and the key to his success and power lay in his great friendship with Charles II. At first this friendship seemed a liability, as John was taken prisoner at the Battle of Worcester in 1651 and spent the next nine years in, first, the Tower of London, and then Warwick Castle.

However, on being released after the Restoration John did not waste much time in establishing his power base. He was appointed Principal Secretary of State for Scotland and he used this as a springboard to acquire a number of other influential posts such as Extraordinary Lord of Session, President of the Council, First Commissioner of the Treasury and Governor of the Castle of Edinburgh. He dealt with any opposition ruthlessly and ruled Scotland as if by divine right. On his marriage to the Countess of Dysart in 1672, he was created Duke of Lauderdale by the King and also a Knight of the Garter.

THE DOORWAY IN THE ANTE-DRAWING ROOM (above). This doorway is an example of the many changes made to the interior of the castle by the architect Sir William Bruce in the 1670s. The swan-pedimented doorcases and the intricate panelling are very much in line with the Duke of Lauderdale's desire for a palatial ambiance. Indeed they are similar to those found at Lauderdale's Surrey villa, Ham House.

Lauder Castle

This Plate Is Most humbly Inscribed to the Rt Honble Charles Earl of Lauderdale &c 1673

It was at this point that he decided Thirlestane was not grand enough for someone of his stature and so commissioned the eminent Scottish architect, Sir William Bruce, to transform Thirlestane into a palace. The result remains one of the most sumptuous creations in Scotland.

Needless to say, with such power he made many enemies: but his friendship with Charles II always saved him. In 1674 a vote by the House of Commons to have him removed from his posts was vetoed by the King and when, four years later, a deputation from Scotland laid 41 separate charges against the Duke, the King, whilst admitting that he might well be guilty, announced: 'I cannot find that he has done anything contrary to my interest.' However when the Duke of York (afterwards James VII) was sent to Scotland in 1680, Lauderdale's influence was finally curbed and by the time of his death in 1683, the only position he had retained was that of Extraordinary Lord of Session.

Further additions to the castle were carried out in 1840, but by the end of the Second World War Thirlestane was in danger of becoming a ruin. Captain the Honourable Gerald Maitland-Carew, who had inherited the castle from his grandfather, the fifteenth Earl of Lauderdale, in 1970, set about a huge rescue operation which had been largely completed by 1982. He has since lived in Thirlestane with his family.

THE DRAWING ROOM (*right*). *The ornate plasterwork was the work of Charles II's 'gentlemen modellers', George Dunsterfield and John Halbert. Charles's master mason Robert Mylne was also employed and the result was some of the finest plasterwork in Europe.*

$\mathcal{B}$EMERSYDE

BEMERSYDE *(left and above). The old tower of Bemersyde was built in 1535, only to be sacked by the English ten years later, during the 'Rough Wooing'. It was repaired in 1585 and gained an extra storey in an attempt to improve the castle's fortifications. The wing to the left (hidden by a tree in the main picture) was added in 1761, while the 24th Laird, James Zerrubabel Haig created the east wing some 35 years later.*

IN THE THIRTEENTH CENTURY True Thomas of Ercildoune, otherwise known as Thomas the Rhymer, wrote: 'Tyde what may, what e'er betyde, Haig shall be Haig of Bemersyde.' On a number of occasions the prophecy has nearly been broken, such as when the 22nd Laird had to sire twelve daughters before he produced a son, but in the end this ancient and most distinguished of families has always managed to find a male heir.

The Haigs' ownership of Bemersyde in fact predates Thomas by at least a century, as is proved by a Charter witnessed by a certain Petrus del Haga of Bemersyde in 1162. They have since been at the forefront of Scottish history: fighting in the Crusades, at Bannockburn, Halidon Hill, Flodden and, in the case of Field Marshal Earl Haig, serving with great distinction in the First World War.

Although there was probably a previous building on the site, the walls of the present tower date from 1535. With Flodden still fresh in the memory, the Scots Parliament passed an Act ordering the Border families to build towers of fortification which could withstand the next inevitable onslaught by the English. Bemersyde, with its eleven-foot thick walls, was specifically erected to guard the Monks-Ford across the Tweed. Ten years later however it proved unequal to the task, as the Earl of Hertford successfully sacked it during the 'Rough Wooing'. It was rebuilt in 1581 and then somehow survived the last two violent decades of the sixteenth century.

When James VI became James I of England in 1603 and finally succeeded in bringing some semblance of peace to the Borders, the Haigs were forced to look elsewhere for their amusement. Having no common enemy left, they and the other Border families took to fighting amongst themselves. James Haig, the seventeenth Laird, was a particularly turbulent character and for a time he was even forced to flee the region after stabbing one of his neighbours during a feud. His brother William took over the estate in 1609 and used his position—King's Solicitor for

FIELD MARSHAL HAIG'S RELICS
*(above). The table in the Field
Marshal's old study is crowded with
signed photographs of the allied
leaders in the Great War. As
Commander in Chief of the British
armies in France, he had an awesome
responsibility and since then has had
many detractors. However there
have been few if any criticisms of his
conduct and leadership from an
officer's most perceptive and
knowledgeable critic—the
private soldier.*

Scotland and Collector of Taxes of the Burghs for the King—to safeguard the family's wealth. But when James returned, it soon transpired that there was no love lost between the brothers either. James claimed that William had committed treason by insinuating that the King was involved in necromancy and together they caused so much trouble that both ended up spending some time in prison in the Tolbooth at Edinburgh. Although they were both later released, James was forced to flee once again in 1620, this time for good, and William was restored to the position of Laird.

Following Charles I's accession to the Scottish throne in 1633, William soon found himself in dispute with the King. He unwisely opposed Charles I's policy regarding the Church in Scotland and in 1634 had to flee to Holland where he died five years later.

As James's eldest son had already died, Robert, the second son, would normally have been in line to inherit the estate. However, not anticipating his brother's premature death, Robert had already forgone his claim and poured his energies into setting up the family whisky firm. (His descendants however regained their rightful inheritance in the nineteenth century.)

Bemersyde therefore passed to his younger brother David and from him to his son Anthony. Anthony, who was Laird from 1654 to 1712, extensively remodelled the tower, building a new roof and using the rafters of the old one as beams for the ground-floor hall. His great-grandson, the 24th Laird, made further changes in 1796, constructing the east wing and adding the battlement to the west wing (built some 35 years earlier).

The direct male line of this branch of the family came to an end when James, the 25th Laird, died unmarried in 1854. The estate was left to his three spinster sisters who spent much of their lives in Rome. As all their possible heirs were female it seemed that finally Thomas's rhyme was to be betrayed—until, that is, fate took a hand. The sisters were in the habit of attending the Scottish church in Rome and one Sunday the Equerry to the then Duke of Edinburgh arrived late and was shown into the only available seat, which happened to be next to their pew. After the service they politely enquired as to his name and were astonished to be told that he was also a Haig. It transpired that he was a direct descendant

THE EARL'S BEDROOM (*right*). *Ever since Bemersyde was first built, this has been the private room or bedroom of the Laird. The main structure, with its stone-vaulted arches, was divided into two levels, with the hall below and this room on the entre sol. The thickness of the walls can today be seen by the depth of the windows, which were inserted later, when the likelihood of an enemy attack had diminished.*

of Robert, the ancestor who had founded the whisky firm two centuries earlier, and he so charmed them that the three sisters resolved to leave him the estate.

Arthur Balfour Haig therefore inherited Bemersyde by deed in 1878 and lived there contentedly right up to the end of the First World War. Indeed it is rumoured that he did not even leave then as recently two neighbours saw a man dressed in Victorian costume ride a massive chestnut horse through a tied-up gate, probably on the way down to the Tweed to catch the 67lb salmon that he reportedly failed to land in 1883.

In 1921 a grateful nation bought Bemersyde and bequeathed it to another descendant of Robert's, Field Marshal Earl Haig. He made the castle more habitable, carrying out extensive repairs to the tower and adding a new staircase block at the rear. He was also responsible for the present garden, including the magnificent sunken garden inspired by the one at Hampton Court. Many of the garden's features date from the distant past. The Spanish Chestnut, said to be 800 years old, was probably brought back by an ancestor from the Crusades. According to family legend it had the dual purpose of being a place from which to hang the Haig enemies and a shady spot to toast the health of visitors. Other objects include a sundial dating from 1690 which now resides in the sunken garden and a statue believed to be of Wattie Eliott, an outlaw from Hermitage Castle. There is said to be a curse on any person who dares move it.

Field Marshal Earl Haig died in 1928 and Bemersyde has since been the home of his son, the thirtieth Laird and second Earl Haig. A renowned painter he has continued with his father's refurbishments and in the process discovered a number of documents concerning the architectural works of his ancestors. One such is the diary of James Zerrubabel Haig, which includes a description of cutting through the eleven-foot-thick tower wall to form an opening for the new east wing and the discovery of a massive rat's nest in the middle of the wall.

Having been witness to more than three centuries of fighting as Scotland strove for its independence, Bemersyde has since enjoyed an even longer period of peace. Throughout this time, indeed for over 800 years, Bemersyde has above all else remained the ancestral home of the Haig family.

WATTIE ELIOT (left). Wattie was a well-known Border outlaw who was always on the run from the authorities. The statue has a curse— that anyone who moves it will die. This was borne out earlier this century, when it was moved from its original position near the west wing and the person responsible duly died.

BEECH WALK *(right). Field Marshal the Earl Haig was responsible for laying out the gardens and woods and, inevitably, the avenue of trees has been planted with military precision. It leads in the direction of the peaceful ruins of Dryburgh Abbey, where the Field Marshal is buried.*

TRAQUAIR IS REPUTEDLY the oldest continuously inhabited house in Scotland and its story is a reflection of eight centuries of political and domestic history. In particular it is a tale concerning that most famous of Scottish families, the Stuarts, who have been Traquair's owners since 1491.

Situated in the heart of what was once Ettrick Forest, Traquair was first built as a royal residence, and by 1107, when Alexander I granted its charter, was in use as a hunting lodge. Towards the end of the thirteenth century it had developed into one of the network of fortified buildings which had grown up along the Tweed valley to guard against an English invasion. It held a strong strategic position on a bend of the River Tweed, but this did not prevent it being occupied by both Edward I and his son Edward II during the Wars of Independence, before being handed over to King Robert the Bruce after his victory at Bannockburn in 1314.

After being leased to a number of different families over the next 150 years, James III's uncle, the Earl of Buchan, used his undoubted influence to acquire Traquair for a paltry sum. He then bestowed it on his son James Stuart, the first Laird, in 1491, and it has remained in the family ever since.

The fourth Laird, Sir John Stuart, was responsible for turning Traquair into a more comfortable dwelling, one fit for his cousin, Mary Queen of Scots, to come and stay. He was also the first member of the family to play a part in public life, being Captain of the Queen's Guard, and later that of James VI (of Scotland).

It was, however, with the seventh Laird, also John, that the family reached the apogee of its political and financial power, only ultimately to begin its fall from grace. Born in the first year of the seventeenth century his rise to public office and honour was swift and spectacular. A favourite of Charles I, he was made the first Earl of Traquair at the age of thirty-three and Lord High Treasurer in 1636. But a year later, when

THE TOP FLOOR *(above). In the sixteenth and seventeenth centuries Mass had to be celebrated in secret, due to the persecution of the Catholics. It was always held at the top of the house in a room commanding a view of all the approaches, so that any unwelcome visitors could be spotted immediately.*

TRAQUAIR HOUSE *(left). Traquair is unique in that its outward appearance has remained practically unaltered for the past 300 years.*

THE CARVED OAK DOOR *(left). The carving symbolizes the conflict between Scotland and England. The unicorn on the left represents Scotland and the lion on the right England. Originally it was in Terreagles House, Dumfriesshire and dates from 1605.*

'THE STEEKIT YETTS' (BEAR GATES) *(left). Legend has it that these gates, completed in 1738, were last opened for Prince Charles Edward Stuart (Bonnie Prince Charlie) during the Jacobite Rising of 1745. When the Prince left after dinner, the fifth Earl wished his guest a safe journey and, on closing the gates, promised that they would not be opened again until the Stuarts had been restored to the throne.*

High Commissioner, he found himself embroiled in the religious disputes surrounding Charles I's attempts to introduce the Revised Prayer Book, so bringing Scotland into line with the Church of England. His attempts to mediate between an obstinate King and an obdurate kirk only led to him being mistrusted by both parties. Out of favour he was soon dismissed from his posts, heavily fined, and forced to retire to his estates. There he carried out a number of improvements, including the diversion of the River Tweed to its present course further north, so as to preserve the house's foundations.

In 1646 he was readmitted to Parliament thanks to Charles I's influence and he enthusiastically rejoined the political fray by signing the Engagement, so joining the Engagers in their support of the King (imprisoned on the Isle of Wight) against Cromwell. His luck did not hold. Following the defeat of the Scots at the Battle of Preston he found himself imprisoned in Warwick Castle. He was released four years later in 1652 and lived in straitened circumstances at Traquair during the Commonwealth. In the last two years of his life he was even seen begging for alms in the streets of Edinburgh and by 1659 was so poor that he 'wanted bread before he died'.

This family tendency to pick the wrong side was unfortunately inherited by his son, the second Earl. He allowed his second wife, Lady Anne Seton, to convert him to Catholicism and this, together with their staunch support of the Jacobites, ensured the family's persecution right up until the Emancipation Act of 1829.

During the last part of the seventeenth century and the first part of the eighteenth century Traquair became the centre of the Jacobite south. The fourth and fifth Earls, both called Charles, were deeply involved in the 1715 and 1745 Risings respectively, and both were imprisoned for their pains. These events inevitably took their toll on the family's wealth. Its lands, which in the seventeenth century extended over three Border counties, had shrunk to a small fraction of their former size by 1800. Indeed since the beginning of the eighteenth century the only alteration to the house has been the conversion of a ground-floor room into a Catholic chapel in 1829, allowing Mass to be celebrated openly at Traquair for the first time in its history.

It is a miracle that Charles, the eighth Earl, was ever able to create a chapel at all. When he assumed the title on the death of his father in 1827, he inherited, along with the shrunken estates, a legacy of debt created by the reckless investments of his forebears in foreign enterprises. He was a shy and eccentric man and, much to his family's despair, a confirmed bachelor. Indeed it is said that he got so tired of his family's attempts at matchmaking that 'he deterred likely female suitors by placing stinging nettles in their beds.' He died childless in 1861 and with him the Earldom became extinct.

His sister, the redoubtable Lady Louisa Stuart, survived until 1875, just short of her hundredth birthday, and her ghost has been seen walking along the banks of the Quair, perhaps waiting to celebrate her centenary. Following her death, Traquair then passed to a cousin, the Honourable Henry Maxwell Stuart, the sixteenth Laird, and has been handed down through his direct descendants until the present day.

Now Traquair is the home of his great-great-granddaughter Catherine Maxwell Stuart, the twenty-first Lady, and her mother Flora and it remains, at least on the outside, much as it was nearly 300 years ago. It is, in the words of Peter, the twentieth Laird, 'A living symbol in stone and mortar of lost causes.'

LORD TRAQUAIR'S BELL (*above*). *This bell harks back to the time when the Stuarts could summon their servants at the pull of a cord.*

MARY QUEEN OF SCOTS' BED *(right).*
This bed, which was originally at
Terreagles House, is now in the
King's room at Traquair. It is said to
be the one in which Mary Queen of
Scots spent her last night in Scotland
before fleeing to England to seek
help from her cousin Queen
Elizabeth I. The only help she
received was to be imprisoned for
eighteen years and then beheaded.

FERNIEHIRST (*left*). *The original tower of Ferniehirst was dismantled on the orders of James VI and the castle as it is today was built by Sir Andrew Kerr, who had been knighted by Mary Queen of Scots. The turnpike stair in the angle is one of the few anti-clockwise turnpike stairs in Scotland, specially designed to suit the left-handed Kerrs.*

·Ferniehirst·

Situated above the River Jed, two miles south of Jedburgh, Ferniehirst was first constructed in 1470 by Sir Thomas Kerr. Although the castle was sacked on a number of occasions, once so badly that it had to be completely rebuilt, it has remained the property of the Kerr family ever since.

The Kerrs, whose name has also been spelt Ker and Carr, were a Norman family who came to Scotland with the De Bruys, the ancestors of Robert the Bruce. By the time of Sir Thomas the family was already well established in the Borders and had been involved in numerous skirmishes with the English. These continued during the sixteenth century and the castle was stormed in 1523 and again during the 'Rough Wooing' in 1544. Sir Thomas died in 1545, but not before valiantly repelling the English at the nearby Battle of Ancrum Moor. Four years later however the English occupied Ferniehirst and it took a combined Scots and French force to drive them out. The English garrison were then apparently butchered in a most barbarous way, even by the standards of those days and the victory is still commemorated every year when the 'Ba Game' is played in Jedburgh. The ball used in the game is meant to represent the head of an English soldier.

In the mid-1560s the title and estates were inherited by another Sir Thomas, who was renowned for the loyal support he offered Mary Queen of Scots. Unhappily for him the only tangible result of his endeavours was the destruction of Ferniehirst and a total of fourteen years' banishment.

One of Sir Thomas's first acts was to lease his house in Jedburgh to Mary in 1565 and it was from there that she rode to Hermitage Castle and back in a day (to meet Lord Bothwell, later to be her husband), nearly dying from pneumonia as a result. In 1570 he raided south to help Mary, with his brother-in-law, Sir Walter Scott of Buccleuch, but was repulsed by the Duke of Sussex who then followed them back to the Borders to wreak vengeance—particularly on Ferniehirst.

THE CHAPEL DOOR (above). The distinctive door to the chapel was built by Sir Andrew Kerr in 1622, after he was created Lord Jedburgh. The quoins and architraves are thought to be unique in Scotland and are reminiscent of Renaissance architecture, which was still prevalent at the time.

Undeterred Sir Thomas set off to Stirling with the intention of taking prisoner the members of the Scottish Parliament. Needless to say he failed and diverted to Edinburgh to help defend Edinburgh Castle on behalf of the Queen. They held out for two years, but in the end had to give in to the superior forces of the Regent Morton. Unlike many of his co-conspirators Sir Thomas escaped execution and instead received a prison sentence, followed by banishment to Flanders.

Sir Thomas was allowed to return to Scotland six years later and in 1581 even had his estates restored to him by James VI. But in 1584 he was banished yet again, this time to Aberdeen where he died a year later.

In 1591 Ferniehirst was dismantled completely on the orders of James VI and Sir Thomas's son Andrew had to wait seven years before he was granted permission to rebuild it. He at first limited himself to reconstructing the tower. However on becoming Lord Jedburgh some 24 years later, in 1622, he added a chapel and the Great Hall to the north of the tower. By this time Border warfare was to all intents over and, as is illustrated by the Great Hall's large windows, the castle was built to admit light now that the need for defence had lessened.

The title and estates continued to pass from father to son until the third Lord Jedburgh died childless. They were then inherited by a cousin, the Fourth Earl of Lothian, who had the distinction of being a Kerr twice over—his father William being the son of Sir Robert Kerr, the Earl of Ancram, and his mother another Kerr cousin, the Countess of Lothian. The fourth Earl was one of the Scottish nobles who invited William of Orange to take the Scottish Crown in 1688 and received the title of Marquis for his support.

Since then the family has continued to distinguish itself. The ninth Marquis served as Secretary of State for Scotland while the eleventh was Secretary to Lloyd George and then Ambassador to Washington in the Second World War. As they owned a number of other houses, Ferniehirst was for a time leased out. Then at the end of the last century it was renovated for use by the Lothian heir. However when he died in a shooting accident it remained empty until the Scottish Youth Hostel Association took it over from 1934 to 1985. It has since become once again the home of the Marquis and Marchioness of Lothian who have carried out many extensive renovations.

THE RED BOY (*above*). *Sir Robert Kerr fought for the Royalists during the Civil War and was forced to flee to Amsterdam, bankrupting his estate. By the time of his death he was so destitute that his creditors claimed his corpse. However his old enemy Oliver Cromwell intervened and persuaded the Dutch to give him a decent burial.*

THE LIBRARY (right). This circular room, leading off the great hall, has always been used as a library. It has recently been restored under the direction of the Marchioness of Lothian and the architect James Simpson and now contains a comprehensive collection of books on the history of the Kerr family worldwide.

·𝒟RUMLANRIG·

ONCE DESCRIBED AS 'the most glorious residence in the British Isles', Drumlanrig is an extraordinary cross between the palace of a sophisticated grandee and the defensive castle of a warrior chief. It sits on a hill (drum) at the end of a long (lang) ridge (rig), and its creator was William Douglas, the first Duke of Queensberry, who devoted twelve years of his life (1679–91) to its construction.

Today it is the home of one of the most distinguished families in Scotland, the Montagu Douglas Scotts—otherwise known as the Dukes of Buccleuch and Queensberry. But originally Drumlanrig was simply a Douglas stronghold.

A charter dating from 1356 reveals that the Barony of Drumlanrig was the property of the Earls of Mar. In 1388 it passed to William Douglas, who became first Laird of Drumlanrig. Remarkably, Drumlanrig then passed from father to son for thirteen successive generations, right up to the death of Charles, third Duke of Queensberry, 400 years later.

DRUMLANRIG AND THE LOWTHER HILLS (left). *The castle lies to the north of Dumfries, by the River Nith—a site of considerable strategic importance as it bars the way from the south to the fertile coastal plains of Ayrshire. Two hundred years ago the thick woods surrounding the castle were decimated by the fourth Duke of Queensberry, known also as 'the Rake of Piccadilly', who sold off the timber to pay for the debts caused by his profligate lifestyle. The estates were extensively replanted during the last century, so that Drumlanrig today has once more a thriving rural industry.*

DRUMLANRIG FROM THE SOUTH (left). *The building takes the form of a simple quadrangular courtyard castle, with towers at each angle. Although this may seem to revert to the style of the thirteenth century, Drumlanrig was in fact built at the end of the seventeenth century and incorporates a number of features typical of Renaissance architecture. Today it is the home of the Duke of Buccleuch, whose ancestors have tended the surrounding estates since 1385.*

During that time the family was continually at the forefront of Scotland's political development and retained particularly close links with the Crown. William supported James I of Scotland, even during his captivity in England, and received the reward of a knighthood at James's coronation in 1424. His son and grandson both followed his example, with the latter giving up his life for his King in battle near Lochmaben in 1484, against the Duke of Albany and the Earl of Douglas.

One of the more remarkable members of the family was Sir James Douglas, who was alive during the violence and turmoil of the sixteenth century. Born in 1498, he inherited Drumlanrig after his father died on the battlefield of Flodden in 1513 and went on to outlive his own son, finally dying at the age of eighty. Having tried unsuccessfully to rescue the young James V from their rivals the Red Douglases in 1526, he then prospered under the French rule of the Regent Marie of Guise, receiving first a knighthood and then the Guardianship of the Western Marches in 1553. He broke with family tradition in opposing Mary Queen of Scots at Carberry Hill in 1567 and surprisingly survived to tell the tale, dying peacefully in his bed in 1578.

His great-grandson William reverted to the family's more traditional stance by supporting the Crown. In 1617 he entertained James VI, during the King's sole trip back to Scotland after his succession to the English throne. He was also responsible for restoring the family's slightly ailing fortunes and was created Earl of Queensberry in 1633.

During the Interregnum the family suffered like many others, but on the restoration of Charles II and the succession of William, third Earl of Queensberry, its power increased once again. Born in 1637, William's ascent to a position of wealth and influence was, to say the least, rapid. He was made a member of the Privy Council in 1667 and then the positions of Justice General, Lord High Treasurer of Scotland and Governor of Edinburgh Castle followed in quick succession. By 1684, when he was made Duke of Queensberry, he had even found favour with the Catholic Stuarts despite his firm Episcopalian views and, under them, became the most powerful man in Scotland.

However, twelve of the last sixteen years of his life were dominated by a project totally removed from politics: the construction of Drumlanrig. The result is there for all to see, a glorious mixture of castle and palace,

THE DOMED ROOFS (*right*). *The domed roof of the clock tower, surrounded by a crown, is similar to that at Holyrood Palace. The ogee domed towers behind are in the angles of the courtyard and each contain a turnpike stair. Under the clock is the date when it was completed, five years before the castle itself was finished.*

created lovingly with a quality of workmanship that it would be difficult to surpass. It is, in a word, unique: the last example of a courtyard castle to be built in Scotland and, at the same time, one of the earliest houses to be designed in the classical Renaissance style.

But when the castle was eventually completed, William was so appalled at the tremendous cost that he could not bring himself to live there and spent only one night at Drumlanrig before his death in 1695.

He was succeeded by his son James, who became famous as the 'Union Duke'. James, who inherited much of his father's political acumen, earned his nickname by not only drawing up the Act of Union between Scotland and England, but also by forcing it through the Scottish Parliament against bitter opposition. The result was the abolition of separate parliaments for England and Scotland and the formation of Great Britain in 1707.

His son Charles, the third Duke, was best known for marrying the vivacious Katherine Hyde—patroness of John Gay, the author of *Beggars' Opera*—who was banned from Court for trying to put on a John Gay play considered too lewd for public presentation. Both of Charles's sons predeceased him, so on his death in 1778 the title passed to a cousin William, known as 'Old Q' and also by many other rather less salubrious nicknames such as 'The Rake of Piccadilly'. William never married but instead spent his time seducing young girls and stripping the Drumlanrig estates of whatever timber and other assets that he could get hold of to pay for his profligacy. Unluckily for the family fortune he somehow lived to the age of 85, and upon his death in 1810 left what little remained of his fortune to his illegitimate daughter, who founded the Wallace Collection and later became the Marchioness of Hertford and a mistress of George IV.

The title of Queensberry and the estates of Drumlanrig (which were entailed) passed to Lady Jane Douglas, the daughter of the second Duke of Queensberry, and it was through her marriage to Francis Scott that the Douglas and Scott families became united.

The Scotts are a famous border family dating back to the time of King David I in the early twelfth century. They were granted the Earldom of Buccleuch by James VI in 1619 and were such fervent Royalists that Francis, the second Earl, was fined what was in those days the crippling

CANON SPOUT *(above). Canon spouts have long been a feature of Scottish architecture and are varied in design and detail. This one, a hippotamus, shows a greater knowledge of the African continent in the seventeenth century than is commonly supposed.*

IRONWORK *(above). This is the crest of the Douglases, a crown over a winged heart. This stems from the time when Sir James Douglas was given the task of taking Robert the Bruce's heart to the Holy Land. On the way he and his men were involved in a fight with the Infidels in Spain. Surrounded by the enemy, Sir James threw the casket containing the King's heart into their midst, shouting 'Forward', and then plunged after it to his death.*

THE NORTH FACADE *(right). With its domed cupola, horseshoe stair and arches in the lower colonnade, this facade shows Renaissance architecture at its best. Although the architect is unknown, the style is based on plans prepared by William Wallace, and the work was supervised by James Smith, who had been responsible for the front of Holyrood House.*

sum of £15,000 by Oliver Cromwell. Francis died in 1651 at the age of twenty-five leaving two young daughters. The eldest soon died while the youngest, Anne, found herself married off by her mother at the age of twelve to the Duke of Monmouth, the fourteen-year-old son of Charles II and Lucy Walters. Although her husband was executed in 1685 for revolting against his uncle James VII, Anne was allowed to retain the title of Duchess of Buccleuch that Charles II had bestowed upon her and continued to live in royal splendour at Dalkeith Palace, which she reconstructed, until her death in 1732.

It was her grandson Francis who married Jane Douglas and both of their titles and estates were then passed down to their grandson Henry who became the third Duke of Buccleuch and the fifth Duke of Queensberry. He was married to the only surviving child of the Duke of Montagu and thus the estates of three great families were united.

Henry died in 1812 and his son outlived him by only seven years, but his grandson, Walter Francis Montagu Douglas Scott, fifth Duke of Buccleuch and seventh Duke of Queensberry, proved to be a fitting heir and consolidated the fortunes of the three families. He also had the foresight to replant the woodlands so devastated by 'Old Q', with the result that Drumlanrig is now, once again, a thriving rural estate.

The remarkable collection of paintings and furniture to be found inside Drumlanrig today is in a large part due to the merger of three such wealthy families: and the collection has been further enhanced by the closure of two of the families' other homes—Montagu House and Dalkeith Palace—earlier this century. On the walls are paintings by Holbein, Leonardo da Vinci and Rembrandt, all of which came from the Montagu family. Priceless pieces of furniture include a cabinet made for Versailles in 1675 and given to Charles II by Louis XIV. Charles in turn gave it to his illegitimate son, the Duke of Monmouth, upon his marriage to Anne, the daughter of the second Earl of Buccleuch, and thus it found its way into the family collection.

If the first Duke of Queensberry could see his creation today one cannot help feeling that he would now believe the original cost amply justified. Quite apart from providing a home for his descendants over the past three hundred years the castle and the possessions inside it are a museum of Scotland's cultural heritage.

THE STAIRCASE *(right). This staircase was added at a later date than the rest of the castle, when the turnpike stairs in the angles of the courtyard became impractical. The portraits at the top of the stairs include one of the second Duke of Queensberry, the 'Union Duke', who forced the Treaty of Union through the Scottish Parliament in 1707. At the bottom of the stairs are some of the family's collection of Old Master paintings.*

·KELBURN·

As FAR BACK as the twelfth century a Boyle or, as they were then called, de Boyville, was in residence at Kelburn. Since then they have fought for Alexander III, Robert the Bruce, James III and Mary Queen of Scots, gained an Earldom, gone bankrupt and served loyally in the Royal Navy for five successive generations. Throughout this time—except from 1488–92 when their lands were attainted by James IV—Kelburn has remained their home.

The Boyles were originally granted the lands of Kelburn in 1140 by their relation Hugh de Morville, the Hereditary High Constable of Scotland. The oldest known part of Kelburn which survives today is the tower constructed by John Boyle, the first Baron of Fairlie, in 1581. It is suspected however that this was simply an enlargement of another tower built in 1140, which would make Kelburn one of the oldest inhabited castles in Scotland. John was an ardent supporter of Mary Queen of Scots and indeed raised a force 100 strong, who fought for her valiantly right up to her defeat at Langside and subsequent flight to England and imprisonment.

The family rose to prominence through David Boyle, later to become the first Earl of Glasgow. A supporter of the Glorious Revolution of William and Mary, he was one of the signatories of the Association for the Defence of William III following the massacre of Glencoe in 1692. He was rewarded by being made a Privy Councillor and Lord of the Treasury and, in addition, he collected the personal titles of Lord Boyle in 1699 and Viscount of Kelburn and Earl of Glasgow in 1703. His prowess as a lawyer and friendship with such influential figures as the Duke of Queensberry ensured his rapid ascent to even greater heights. He was appointed High Commissioner to the General Assembly of the Church of Scotland in 1706 and lent his considerable professional expertise to the preparation of the Treaty of Union with England.

KELBURN (*left*). *Kelburn, which overlooks the Firth of Clyde, has been owned by the Boyle family since 1140. The oblong tower, incorporating parts of an earlier castle, dates from 1581 and the corner stair-towers were added later for greater comfort. In the early eighteenth century the first Earl of Glasgow built the wing to the left of the photograph and in the last century a further wing was added. Finally, at the end of the nineteenth century, the seventh Earl of Glasgow built an extension of corrugated iron to house his servants—a unique example of a tin shed forming part of an ancestral home.*

However, all his brilliance could not overcome the general antipathy felt towards his friendship with another famous character, the Earl of Mar. Suspected of harbouring Jacobite sympathies, he was forced to resign from public office in 1714. He attempted to ingratiate himself with the Hanoverian Government by offering to maintain 1000 men at his own expense and indeed he subsequently helped to raise 6000 men at Irvine. But the animosity that had built up against him ran too deep and, deprived of any position of power, he busied himself with the running of his estate until his death in 1733.

For the next century and a quarter the affairs of the Boyle family and of Kelburn ran smoothly. While none reached the illustrious heights of their forebear they upheld the family name with honour and dignity. However on the death of the fifth Earl in 1869 and the succession of his half brother, some thirty years his junior, disaster struck.

The sixth Earl spent his early years at Oxford and became deeply involved in the Pre-Raphaelite Movement, the Gothic Revival and various controversial religious sects. Upon inheriting the title and the vast amount of wealth that accompanied it, he decided to dispose of the latter through becoming a great religious benefactor. Within a couple of years he had set into motion a vast programme of church building all over Scotland. Kelburn itself gained a new wing, probably designed by the Victorian architect Butterfield and to this day its interior has retained the Pre-Raphaelite influence of William Morris.

Inexorably he built his way through the family fortune until, by 1888, he had not only bankrupted all of his various estates, but also run up debts in excess of a million pounds. All the estates, houses and furniture had to be put up for sale and Kelburn itself was only saved when his cousin and heir sold his own estates at Shewalton and just raised sufficient funds to buy the castle. Unsurprisingly the sixth Earl is not remembered with much affection by the family and when he died in 1890 his portrait was banished to an obscure part of the castle.

For the following generations life has been a never ending struggle to make ends meet. Their chosen career, service in the Royal Navy, has brought them honour, but has not been particularly conducive to the creation of wealth. Patrick, the tenth and present Earl, has turned Kelburn into a country centre which he now successfully manages.

WILLIAM AND MARY WING *(above).*
Completed in 1722, this wing is a rare example of this style of architecture in Scotland. Set at an oblique angle to the old tower, the thick walls had to be quarried through to connect the new building. To the left is a later wing, designed by the Victorian architect Butterfield, whose pupil, William Morris, designed the wallpaper and fittings in the dining room.

THE DRAWING ROOM (*right*). *This room formed part of the new wing designed by the first Earl of Glasgow, whose portrait hangs over the fireplace. The room was previously the dining room, but with changing habits of hospitality the importance and sequence of rooms were changed.*

CASSILIS *(left). The word Cassilis is derived from the Gaelic 'Caisial', which means fort. The castle dates from the fourteenth century and the walls are between sixteen and twenty-foot thick at the base. They become progressively thinner the higher the building rises, but are still ten-foot thick on the third floor.*

WHEN JOHN KENNEDY OF DUNURE killed Dalrymple and so saved Marjorie de Montgomerie from Dalrymple's evil clutches, he not only gained a grateful spouse but also a new home, Cassilis Castle. Since that time, in the mid-fourteenth century, the castle has remained the property of the Kennedys, a family deeply involved in the political intrigue which so typifies Scotland's history.

The first Kennedy to rise to a position of prominence was John's great-grandson. In 1452 he was created a peer of Scotland by James II and, on the latter's death, became one of the six Regents of Scotland during the minority of James III.

This link to the Stuart dynasty was further strengthened over the next two generations. The second Lord Kennedy was a Councillor to James III, and his daughter, Janet, one of the many mistresses of James IV. Indeed her influence undoubtedly contributed to her half-brother David, the third Lord Kennedy, becoming Earl of Cassilis in 1509.

The political power of the Kennedys reached its peak during the life of Gilbert, the third Earl of Cassilis. He led a particularly active life, constantly switching his allegiance between the English and the Scots.

He inherited the title at the age of twelve and his first act (two months later) was to sign, under duress, the death warrant of Patrick Hamilton, the first Protestant martyr. He completed his education in France and his knowledge of the language stood him in good stead when he was sent there in 1535 as one of the ambassadors arranging the short-lived marriage of James V to the French King's daughter. In 1542 he had the misfortune to be captured by the English at the defeat of Solway Moss. He only secured his release from prison by giving as hostages his uncle and two of his brothers and by agreeing to support Henry VIII in his wish to marry the future Edward VI to Mary Queen of Scots.

When this marriage failed to materialize, the King demanded he return to England to complete his sentence. Gilbert however declined the offer and left his relatives languishing in his place. Despite his

VIEW FROM THE FRONT *(above). It was from a small room at the top of the tower that the wife of the sixth Earl is reputed to have watched her lover, Johnny Faa, and fourteen other gypsies being hanged from a tree by her husband. Today called the Countess's Room, it is said to be haunted by her to this day.*

tendency to divide his loyalties Gilbert somehow regained the favour of the King, secured the release of his relatives and indeed acted as Henry VIII's ambassador in negotiating a conciliation with the Scots. This came to naught and Gilbert defected once again to the Scottish side.

In 1558 he was one of the eight Commissioners to go to France for the marriage of Mary Queen of Scots to the Dauphin and it was during this trip that his political wiles finally deserted him. Along with the other Commissioners he refused to grant the Scottish Crown Matrimonial to the Dauphin (recognizing him as King of Scotland), which caused such offence to the French that some of the Commissioners, including Gilbert, were poisoned before they could leave France.

His successor, Gilbert the fourth Earl of Cassilis, is chiefly remembered for the particularly gruesome way in which he acquired the Abbey of Crossraguel. The Abbey had been promised to him by his Uncle Quentin, but for his ownership to be official he still needed the consent of the Commendator, Allan Stewart. He therefore invited the latter to dinner and asked him to honour Quentin's promise and sign over the Abbey lands. When Stewart refused to do so (he was trying to feather his own nest by agreeing terms with another party) the Earl summoned his butler, cook and pantryman to take the luckless Commendator down to the dungeon, where a large fire was blazing. The Commendator was stripped, had his arms and legs tied and, after being basted in oil so that 'the roast should not burn', was hung over the fire. It is said that he was half-roasted by the time he agreed to sign the papers.

The Commendator later escaped with the help of Kennedy of Bargany and promptly revoked all he had been forced to sign, but this did not prevent Gilbert obtaining the legal ownership of the lands shortly before his death in 1576.

The sixth and seventh Earls, both zealous Protestants, were firm in their support of Parliament and although they suffered for their beliefs, the estates remained largely intact. The eighth Earl died childless in 1759 and the title then passed through a number of cousins before ending up with Archibald, the twelfth Earl, who was made Marquess of Ailsa in 1832 for his political services.

Cassilis was leased out for a time during this century until David, the present and seventh Marquess, moved in with his wife Mary in 1956.

WALL PAINTING *(above). Positioned at the entrance to the Laird's private apartments, this painting was designed to dissuade servants from entering the apartments. It dates from 1456 and the words mean 'Come not near master porter'.*

THE TURNPIKE STAIR *(right)*. *This is
one of the few examples in Scotland
of a turnpike stair with a hollow
newel post. Built by the seventh
Laird in about 1690, this stair is
particularly unique as there is room
for a man to climb up within the
hollow. It ascends in a clockwise
direction, so that the right-handed
defender could hold onto the rail
with his left hand as he backed up
the stairs, leaving his sword hand
free to fight off any pursuers.*

CRAUFURDLAND

CRAUFURDLAND CASTLE is the home of the Houison Craufurds, the proud upholders of the traditional ceremony of *Servitium Lavacri*, whereby they bathe the hands of every King or Queen of the United Kingdom upon their accession to the throne.

Their ancestry can be traced back to Sir Reginald de Craufurd, Sheriff of Ayrshire, who established the family fortune by marrying the Loudoun heiress in about 1200. On his death his estates were divided up among his sons, one of whom, John, became the first Laird of Craufurdland.

Craufurdland's ideal defensive position, overlooking the Fenwick Water which stretches out in the valley below, suggests that a keep must have been there from the earliest times. It was the base from which the Craufurd ancestors made their glorious sorties onto the field of battle. Family records relate that the third Laird helped his cousin Sir William Wallace become Warden of Scotland in 1297 and that the seventh Laird fought valiantly against the English in France at the siege of Creyult in 1423, for which he was awarded a knighthood by James I.

Craufurdland as it stands today is the result of three different stages of construction. The first, dated to the early sixteenth century, was the tower, which was probably built on the foundations of a previous keep. Though sufficiently spacious when it was built, the sixteenth Laird, who was alive a century and a half later, found conditions in the tower rather cramped for himself and his twelve offspring and so constructed a new, detached wing to the east of the main block. Although the exact date of its completion is unknown, an elaborately decorated ceiling in the principal bedroom displays the arms of Charles I and the date of 1648, the year before Charles's execution.

The generations who followed the sixteenth Laird performed on the field of battle with as much distinction as their forebears and none more so than the twentieth Laird, John Walkinshaw Craufurd. A member of the British Army, he proved his worth at Dettingen and Fontenoy.

CRAUFURDLAND BY NIGHT *(left)*. *Craufurdland, near Kilmarnock, stands on a bluff of land overlooking the Fenwick Water. The oldest part of the castle is to the right of the photograph, and is thought to have been built on the foundation of an older castle in the sixteenth century. As the family grew, so did the castle; the crow-stepped building to the left was built in the seventeenth century and further additions to the right were made a hundred years later. Finally, in 1825, the castle was enlarged in accordance with the fashion of the time.*

THE CHARLES I BEDROOM *(above).*
This room forms part of the
additions made to Craufurdland in
the seventeenth century. Its ornate
plastered ceiling incorporates the
arms of Charles I and the date when
the work was finished, 1648 — one
year before Charles was beheaded.

However, following the Jacobite Rising of 1745, he found his loyalties split between the Government and his great friend the Earl of Kilmarnock, who had been found guilty of treason (for being a Jacobite) and given the death sentence. Risking his career in the army, John showed true Scottish grit in escorting his friend to the scaffold, holding the corner of the cloth which received his severed head and then ensuring that the Earl received a proper burial. This flagrant breach of conduct threatened to damage his army career irretrievably, but such was his ability that he rose again to become a Major Commandant and then a Lieutenant Colonel. His rehabilitation was complete in 1761 when he was appointed Falconer to the King for Scotland.

John never married and indeed had a reputation of being a misogynist. This was borne out by his will, in which he ignored the claims of an aunt—his closest relation—and instead settled the entire estate on the London banker, Sir Thomas Coutts. His aunt, Elizabeth Houison, proved equal to the challenge however, as she successfully contested the will and so united the families of Houison and Craufurd.

For the Craufurds this union brought not only the Houison name and estates of Braehead, but also the Houison family legend: and it is from this that the ceremony of *Servitium Lavacri* has its origins. Tradition has it that James II, while travelling on his own in the disguise of a common peasant, was set upon by a gang of ruffians near Cramond Bridge by Edinburgh. A certain Jock Houison, who happened to be passing, rescued the King without realizing who he was and took him to his home to attend to the King's wounds. In gratitude the King invited the bemused Jock to drop in on him at Edinburgh Castle—asking for 'Ane James Stewart'.

Walter Scott included the story in his *Tales of a Grandfather* and later decided that George IV's visit to Holyrood in 1822 provided the perfect opportunity for the event to be commemorated. He therefore arranged for Jock's descendant, William Houison Craufurd (Elizabeth Houison's grandson), to be in attendance, with a silver basin for George IV to wash his hands.

This 'Act of Service' now happens at the beginning of each reign and it is theoretically performed in return for the Laird's continued tenure of his property. The present Laird, Peter Houison Craufurd, has himself

THE MAIN HALL *(right). This hall forms part of the massive central tower, built in 1825, linking the other parts of the castle together. Its creator was the first Houison Craufurd to perform the ceremony of* Servitium Lavacrii.

twice been present at the ceremony—after the accession of both George VI and the present Queen. However he now devotes his time not to the washing of hands but to the family firm, which deals in game and smoked products as well as the rearing of guinea fowl. In this task he is assisted by his wife Caroline and his eldest son.

As for Craufurdland Castle itself, it has recently been restored to something like its past condition with the help of a grant from the Historic Buildings Council for Scotland.

· CAPRINGTON ·

TRADITION HAS IT that a forebear of the Cunynghams, the owners of Caprington since 1425, once saved the life of Malcolm, the future King of Scotland. He was peacefully making hay on a beautiful summer's afternoon at the beginning of the eleventh century when Malcolm, the son of Macduff, stumbled up to him begging for a place to hide from the murderous Macbeth. The quick-thinking Cunyngham bade him slip into a half-completed haystack which he then proceeded to heap higher and higher. The ruse succeeded as by the time Macbeth arrived, Malcolm was out of sight and Cunyngham was unconcernedly creating another stack.

The first connection between the Cunynghams and Caprington was in 1425, when Adam Cunyngham married the daughter of Sir Duncan Wallace, the heiress of Caprington, and so became the first Cunyngham Laird. The family also held the position of Coronership which was a source of considerable income.

The first Laird's great-grandson John was still a minor when he first inherited the castle and the Coronership and when the Montgomeries questioned his rights to the latter they unwittingly started a feud that was to continue for eighty years.

With the death of James V in 1542, John entered the world of politics, siding with Cardinal Beaton and the Queen Dowager, Mary of Guise. He raised the men and money needed to capture the Castle of Yester from the English in 1548 and four years later assembled a force of infantry to fight in France. His military ventures did not come cheap and in 1556 he was even forced, temporarily, to sell the farm at Caprington.

John's son William, the fifth Laird, continued the feud with the Montgomeries, although mainly through the courts. Most of his time, however, was taken up with keeping his own relations out of trouble.

In spite of all this and the presence of a bastard son, William was made High Commissioner to the Church of Scotland in 1581, the first and only commoner to be so appointed until this century.

CAPRINGTON CASTLE (*left*). *Caprington was built in the fifteenth century on a ten-foot-high outcrop of rock beside the River Irvine. It originally consisted of the rectangular tower seen here and a staircase tower on the other side. Its present appearance owes much to the major alterations carried out in 1820.*

THE TOP OF THE STAIRCASE *(left)*. *The main staircase was remodelled in 1820 by the architect P. Wilson. Due to the natural contours of the ground, he had to build a steep flight of stairs leading up onto the rock platform on which the original tower had been constructed.*

The family name was further enhanced two generations later by Sir John Cunyngham, later Baronet of Nova Scotia. Born in 1624 he became the MP for Ayrshire and in 1678 was the representative chosen by the Scottish Government to take to London the inventory of 41 grievances against the Duke of Lauderdale. Although it did not lead to the Duke's immediate demise it certainly added weight to the body of opinion against him, and when the Duke was forced to stand down Sir John was offered the Chancellorship in his place. He however was unable to accept the appointment on account of ill health.

When Sir John died in 1683, his nineteen-year-old son William inherited the title and estates. Unfortunately for him there were also debts amounting to at least £92,000 and no less than 27 dependants to support. Despite marrying an heiress, William's life was, by his own account, one long struggle against an ever mounting burden of debt.

His grandson succeeded him but died childless and so Caprington passed to a female cousin, Anne. She married John Smith, an Edinburgh lawyer and changed her name to Smith-Cunningham and it is from them that the seventeenth and present Laird, Captain Robert Cunyngham, is descended.

SUIT OF ARMOUR (right). The arms and armour displayed on the wall are reminders of the turbulent past that this part of Scotland experienced. The last battle to be fought nearby was Bothwell Brig in 1679, when the Covenanters were defeated by Charles II's illegitimate son, the Duke of Monmouth.

Acknowledgement

The research and preparation of any book dealing with families, their history and their castles is only possible with the help and advice of many people. This book is no exception.

First and foremost I would like to thank the owners for allowing me to include their homes and for their hospitality, help and kindness—as well as patience—in correcting my drafts.

The compilation of a preliminary list was aided by friends and was then checked by Sir Malcolm Innes of Edingight, the Lord Lyon King of Arms, for whose knowledge I am most grateful.

Sources on the architecture and history included the works of Nigel Tranter, Harry Gordon Slade, John Prebble and a variety of biographies and histories in the London Library.

I received help from *Country Life*, *The Field* and *Scottish Field* in tracing back numbers featuring various castles. The following also gave me a great deal of their valuable time: Hilary Williams of the British Museum, Peter Sinclair of the Historic Houses Association, David Walker and members of the staff of Historic Scotland, Iain Brown of the National Library of Scotland, Helen Watson of the National Portrait Gallery of Scotland, Isla Robertson of the National Trust for Scotland and Jane Thomas of the Royal Commission on the Ancient and Historical Monuments of Scotland.

Many friends gave me bed and board, advice, support and checked my preliminary notes. These included Sonagh Asplin, Bruce and Sheila Bell, Duncan and Gilly Bengough, Charles Boyle, Patrick Cardwell Moore, Jan and Sally Collins, Charles de Salis, Marybelle Drummond, Sheila Fairbairn, Robin and Diana Freemantle, Carl Josef Henckel von Donnersmarck, Angus and Ashie Hildyard, Roy Keith, James and Diana Lindsay, Justin Lowinsky, Colin and Jenny MacGregor, Nigel and Joyce Porter, Miff and Zilla Tuck, Hazel Wager and Peter Wise. I apologize to those who have been equally helpful and have been omitted. They are the victims of my poor memory.

A special vote of thanks goes to Elizabeth McLeod who had to decipher my manuscripts and type up the drafts in a legible form. Sam Lloyd was given a difficult assignment, which was often in the laps of the weather gods. His photographs have proved that it was worth dashing out halfway through lunch to catch the fleeting rays of the sun.

I must also thank Mark Collins, who was introduced to me by Jenny Maclean, the staff at Collins and Brown for their support and especially Colin Ziegler who edited the book with such good humour.

Lastly my thanks would be due to Frances Farquharson, were she still alive, as it was she who decided that I should turn my hand to writing and thus it is to her memory that this book is dedicated.

CHRONOLOGY

The Forming of a Nation

A.D.

84 The Battle of Mons Graupius near Inverness—the northernmost point of the Roman invasion against the Caledonian tribes.

409 The Roman Army leaves Britain. Scotland in four realms. Picts in the north-east to the Forth, Angles in the south-east and Northumbria. The Celtic Britons in the Kingdom of Strathclyde and Cumbria and the Gaelic Scots from Ireland in the Kingdom of Dalriada on the west coast.

563 St Columba arrives in Iona from Ireland. He helps spread Celtic Christianity.

800 The Norwegians start to raid and finally settle the north and western coasts.

843 Kenneth McAlpin of Dalriada defeats the Picts and forms the Kingdom of Scotia or Alba, with his capital in Fortevoit, Perthshire.

1018 Malcolm II defeats the Angles at Carham on the Tweed.

1034 Malcolm II's grandson, Duncan I, becomes King of a united Scotland.

1057 Duncan I's son, Malcolm Canmore, kills Macbeth and becomes King of Scots.

The Years of Prosperity

1072 William the Conqueror invades and makes Malcolm III (Canmore) pay homage at Abernathy, Perthshire. Malcolm moves the capital to Edinburgh.

1124 William's ninth son David I grants estates in Scotland to his Anglo-Norman friends, who introduce feudal administration and Norman architecture.

1164 Somerled, King of the Isles, is killed attacking Glasgow. His successors are styled Lord of the Isles.

1165 William the Lion concludes an alliance with France.

1174 William is captured and forced to sign the Treaty of Falaise, subjecting Scotland to England.

1189 The Treaty of Falaise is renounced on payment of 10,000 marks to Richard Coeur de Lion.

1214 Alexander II is crowned and gives up his claims to Northumbria and Cumbria.

1263 Alexander III defeats the Norwegians at the Battle of Largs. The Hebrides are returned to Scotland.

1286 Alexander III is succeeded by his granddaughter, the Maid of Norway, who dies on her way from Norway to become Queen and marry Edward I's son.

1291 Edward I asked to adjudicate between the thirteen rival claimants for the Scottish Crown and selects John de Balliol in preference to Robert de Bruce.

The Wars of Independence

1296 Balliol refuses Edward I's demands, who then invades Scotland and deposes Balliol. He declares Scotland to be his fiefdom, making 2,000 nobles pay homage to him by signing a document called the Ragman Roll.

1297 William Wallace starts the rebellion against English rule, which is crushed by Edward I.

1306 Robert the Bruce is crowned as King of Scots, but is excommunicated for killing his rival John Comyn, of the powerful Buchan family, in a church.

1314 Robert the Bruce defeats the English at the Battle of Bannockburn.

1320 Declaration of Arbroath signed by the nobles asking the Pope to recognize Robert as King and annul his excommunication.

1328 Treaty of Northampton recognizes Scotland as an independent Kingdom and Robert as its King. He dies the following year.

1333	Battle of Halidon Hill. Scots defeated by the English under Edward III who supports Balliol's son for the Crown.
1346	Battle of Neville's Cross. Scots invade England to help the French after their defeat at Crecy and are defeated. David II captured and held prisoner for the next twelve years.
1358	David II released upon the staged payment of 100,000 marks (£66,000) which cripples Scotland's economy.

The Early Stewarts

1371	Robert II, the son of Robert the Bruce's daughter Margaret and Walter Stewart crowned as the first Stewart King.
1388	Battle of Otterburn between the Douglases and the Percys.
1406	The future James I captured on his way to France and is held at the English Court for eighteen years.
1411	The Highland Host is defeated at the Battle of Harlaw in Aberdeenshire.
1422	Battle of Bauge. The English are defeated by the French and Scots.
1424	James I returns to Scotland and reasserts the Crown's authority.
1437	James I is killed by his nobles and is succeeded by James II, who is aged six.
1460	James II killed by a cannon exploding at the siege of Roxburgh Castle and is succeeded by his son, aged nine.
1469	James II marries Margaret, daughter of the King of Denmark and Norway, who brings as her dowry the Orkneys and Shetlands.
1488	James III is killed after the Battle of Sauchieburn, fighting his own son who has the backing of a faction of nobles.
1498	The title Lord of the Isles is assumed by James IV.
1513	James IV, Henry VIII's brother-in-law, is killed at the Battle of Flodden and succeeded by his one-year-old son James V.
1523	The Borders are harried by the English.
1535	The Border Lairds are instructed to fortify their houses.
1542	James V dies after hearing the news of the defeat at Solway Moss and is succeeded by his week-old daughter, Mary Queen of Scots.
1544 –5	The Rough Wooing. Henry VIII tries to force a marriage between his son and Mary Queen of Scots and lays waste to the south of Scotland.

1547	The Scots defeated at the Battle of Pinkie. French troops arrive in Scotland.
1548	Mary Queen of Scots is sent to France for safe-keeping and later marries the Dauphin.
1557	The Lords of the Congregation sign the First Covenant, to set up a reformed national Church.
1558	Elizabeth I becomes Queen of England.
1559	Mary Queen of Scots's husband, Francois II, becomes the King of France.

The Reformation and Mary Queen of Scots

1560	French troops are besieged in Leith. The Regent Marie of Guise dies. The Treaty of Edinburgh is signed whereby all French and English troops are to leave Scotland. The authority of the Pope is abolished and the Reformation proclaimed.
1561	Mary Stuart, Queen of Scots returns to Scotland on the death of her husband Francois II.
1562	Battle of Corrochie. Mary defeats the Catholic Earl of Huntly.
1565	Mary marries Henry Lord Darnley, who is the great-grandson of Henry VII.
1567	Darnley is murdered. Bothwell marries the Queen. At Carberry Hill Bothwell goes into exile and the Queen is held prisoner at Loch Leven Castle. Mary is forced to abdicate in favour of her one-year-old son James.
1568	Mary escapes from Loch Leven, is defeated at Langside and flees to England where she is held prisoner by Elizabeth I.
1573	Edinburgh Castle, held for Queen Mary, is finally surrendered.
1587	Mary Queen of Scots executed at Fotheringhay, Northampton-shire after being in prison for eighteen years.
1594	Battle of Glenlivet between James VI's troops and the Catholic Earls of Huntly and Erroll.
1603	Elizabeth I dies.

The Union of the Crowns

1603	James VI of Scotland crowned in London as James I of England.
1609	The Statute of Iona curtails the power of the Highland Chiefs.

1624 The creation of the Baronetcies of Nova Scotia.

1633 Charles I crowned King of Scotland at Scone.

1638 The signing of the National Covenant, protesting against the Revised Prayer Book.

1642 Outbreak of Civil War in England. The Covenanters send an army to help the Parliamentarians in England.

1645 Montrose raises an army for Charles I and conquers Scotland. He is finally defeated at Philliphaugh and flees abroad.

1649 Charles I beheaded in Whitehall.

1650 Montrose returns and is executed by the Marquess of Argyll. Charles II lands in Scotland. Cromwell defeats the Scots at Dunbar and the following year at Worcester. Charles II escapes abroad after the battle.

1660 The Restoration of Charles II.

1679 Battle of Bothwell Brig. The Royalist Army under Charles II's illegitimate son the Duke of Monmouth defeats the Covenanters.

1688 The Glorious Revolution. William of Orange deposes James VII and II, whose army is led by Graham of Claverhouse (Bonnie Dundee), killed at the Battle of Killiecrankie.

1692 The massacre of Glencoe. The Campbells are ordered to kill the Macdonalds of Glencoe as their chief had delayed taking the oath of allegiance to King William.

1695 The Darien Scheme is launched, to rival the English East India and Africa Companies. Its aim is to control the Darien Isthmus in Central America, used for the shipment of goods to and from India. Its failure almost bankrupts Scotland.

1706 Scottish Commissioners under the Duke of Queensberry sent to London to open negotiations for a Treaty of Union.

The Union of the Parliaments

1707 The Treaty of Union signed. The Scottish and English Parliaments dissolved to form one Parliament at Whitehall with 45 Scottish members in the Commons and 16 representative Scottish peers in the Lords. Scotland and England together form Great Britain.

1714 Queen Anne, the last of the Stuarts, dies. She is succeeded by George I of Hanover.

1715 Jacobite Rising, which fails after the Battle of Sheriffmuir.

1719 Jacobite Rising aided by Spain. Defeated at Battle of Glenshiel.

1745 Jacobite Rising under Prince Charles Edward.

1746 Battle of Culloden. Escape of Prince Charles Edward to France.

1757 Highland Regiments are recruited for the Seven Years War and disbanded in 1763.

1762 Start of the Highland Clearances.

1775 Further recruitment of Highlanders for the American War of Independence.

1782 Disarming Act repealed. Imposed in 1746, it had prohibited the carrying of arms, wearing of the kilt and playing of bagpipes.

1784 Forfeited Jacobite estates are restored to their owners.

1793 Recruitment of Highlanders for the French Wars.

1822 George IV pays the first State visit to Scotland since Charles II.

1846 The start of the potato famines.

1852 Queen Victoria buys Balmoral Castle.

INDEX

The eighteenth Earl had barely inherited the title when he died of fever brought on by his grief at the death of one of his two daughters. His wife had perished a few weeks earlier—apparently from exhaustion after nursing her husband devotedly for twenty-one days and nights without sleep—and so their sole surviving daughter Elizabeth was left alone, heiress to the title and estates at the grand age of one. This however did not appear to hinder her progress in the least as she subsequently married one of England's richest landowners, George Granville Leveson-Gower, the second Marquess of Stafford. And when he was made Duke of Sutherland in 1833, she acquired the unique title of Duchess Countess.

Following a fire in 1785 Elizabeth had taken the opportunity to build the east wing of the castle, but it was her son, the second Duke, who was responsible for the total remodelling of the outside of Dunrobin. Sir James Barry, the designer of the Houses of Parliament, was commissioned to create 'one of the most splendid ducal castles in the United Kingdom' and the result, after five years of work (1845–50), is broadly what we see today. However a fire in the First World War badly damaged the castle and the Scottish architect, Robert Lorimer, rebuilt some of the main rooms as well as reducing the height of the main tower.

The third Duke, who became Britain's largest landowner, married Anne Hay-Mackenzie of Castle Leod and was keen to promote industry in the area, even going so far as to build part of the Highland Railway at his own expense. The fifth Duke showed rather less interest in administrative life, preferring to indulge his great passion for big game hunting. Indeed after the First World War a large part of the Sutherland estates was sold and when he died without children in 1963, the title of Earl of Sutherland and the remainder of the estates passed to his brother's daughter Elizabeth, the present Countess. The Dukedom, being a United Kingdom title, reverted to a descendant of the first Duke's brother and is now no longer associated with Dunrobin.

Following its reconstruction in the nineteenth century Dunrobin Castle today appears, at least on the outside, to be a relatively modern castle. This however belies the old structures still standing within and the seven centuries of Scottish family history that the castle has been witness to.

THE INNER COURTYARD (above). The tower which can be seen through this circular window forms the nucleus of the oldest part of the castle surviving to this day. It was from its top that the head of the eighth Earl's illegitimate son was displayed, after he had unsuccessfully tried to seize the family estates and title.

THE LIBRARY (right). In 1915 part of Dunrobin, at the time in use as a hospital, was destroyed by a fire. Following the Great War, Sir Robert Lorimer, the eminent Scottish architect, was commissioned to carry out repairs and took the opportunity to remodel the interior. The library was just one of the rooms which benefited from the quality of his simple design style. The portrait on the far wall is of Millicent, the daughter of the Earl of Rosslyn and wife of the fourth Duke of Sutherland. She was known as 'Meddlesome Millie' by her English retainers in Staffordshire and, whether this title was justified or not, she did much good work for he Dunrobin and other Sutherland estates.

ALEXANDER, THE TWELFTH EARL
(above). *Alexander was just sixteen
when his parents were poisoned and
he was forced to marry the daughter
of his guardian, the Earl of
Caithness. Caithness tried to have
him murdered so that his daughter
would inherit the estates; but
Alexander managed to escape and
later married Lady Jean Gordon, the
ex-wife of Lord Bothwell.*

·DUNVEGAN·

EVER SINCE LEOD, son of Olaf the Black, built a massive curtain wall around a rocky outcrop on the Isle of Skye in the thirteenth century, Dunvegan Castle (as it became) has remained the principal home and stronghold of the Chiefs of MacLeod, one of the largest clans in the Highlands.

In that time they have won and lost many battles, sold off various properties and lands, and indulged in bloody family feuds: but the central symbol of their power—the castle on the rock—has both grown and prospered.

VIEW OF DUNVEGAN FROM THE SOUTH-WEST *(left). The castle is ...ed on an outcrop of rock which ... originally separated from the ...land by a deep ditch. Right up ...he eighteenth century the only ... to penetrate the outside wall ... to cross Loch Dunvegan itself ...d enter through the Sea Gate.*

HEALAVAL MOOR *(left). This is the site where Alasdair Crotach gave a banquet for James V. On the King's arrival at Dunvegan, he and his party were led to the flat-topped summit of Healaval Moor, where, in the gathering dusk, they found a large banquet laid out on linen. Surrounded by MacLeod clansmen, each holding a blazing faggot under the starlit sky, Alasdair greeted the King thus: 'Here, Sire, is my hall: its walls are great mountains, its roof the canopy of heaven. My table is 2000 feet high and here, bearing the lighted torches, are my priceless sconces and your faithful servants.'*

VIEW OVER LOCH (*left*). *Now, as* *the past, the castle occupies a* *position of great security as well* *beauty. The barracks from whi* *this photograph was taken we* *constructed in 1790 by Norma* *MacLeod. Their purpose was t* *house recruits for the regiment of* *Black Watch that he was raisin* *from his clan at the time.*

Malcolm, the third chief and great-grandson of Leod, was responsible for the keep, the first stone structure to be built inside the Sea Wall. Although it had to be reroofed in 1790 by Norman MacLeod, the twenty-third chief, it has otherwise survived intact. Indeed the dungeon remains in much the same condition as it must have been in the fourteenth century.

The MacLeods played as big a role as any clan in the political chaos and clan feuds which followed James IV's assumption of the title of the Lordship of the Isles in 1498. Alasdair Crotach, the eighth chief, continually had to defend his territory against rival clans and, to this end, built the Fairy Tower on the south-east corner of the Sea Wall.

The period after Alasdair's death (1547) was a black one for the MacLeod clan. His son William soon followed him to the grave leaving an infant daughter as his heiress. The subsequent clan meeting, dissatisfied with the idea of a female leader, selected a third cousin, Malcolm, as chief, but Iain Dubh, another cousin, had different ideas. He slaughtered all his rivals, with the exception of the heiress Mary, who was under the guardianship of the Earl of Argyll, and Norman, Mary's uncle, who had fled to the mainland.

A visiting party of eleven Campbells was sent to Dunvegan to assess Iain Dubh's suitability for the position of clan chief. Iain Dubh invited them to dinner and instead of providing red wine, he had goblets of blood placed before his horrified guests, who were then butchered by their dinner companions.

Both the Earl of Argyll and the Regent Queen Mary decided that this time Iain Dubh had overstepped the mark and they dispatched Hugh Rose of Kilravock to avenge the deaths. Iain Dubh, however, had already fled to Ireland and there he met a suitably violent end when he picked a quarrel with the O'Donnells, who had him disembowelled with red hot irons. This left the way clear for Norman to take over as chief.

Sir Rory Mor, Norman's second son, became the clan's fifteenth chief in 1595. He was to lead the MacLeods through the troubled closing stages of clan warfare into the more settled period under the centralized government of King James VI. In his younger days he was continually in trouble with the authorities, mainly due to a long-standing feud he had with the Macdonalds of Sleat. Many unsuccessful attempts were made

THE FAIRY TOWER (above). This [...] was built by Alasdair Crotach [...] the beginning of the sixteenth [...]. It was constructed on top of [...] original curtain wall (put up by [...] the first chief, at the end of the [...]enth century) and the corbels of [...] old wall can still be seen today.

THE DUNVEGAN CUP (above). In 1594 Rory Mor led 500 MacLeods to Ulster, to help the Irish in a rebellion against Queen Elizabeth. He then ignored James VI's order to return, much to the delight of the Irish, who presented him with the cup as a token of their gratitude.

to negotiate a truce, one of which proved to be particularly disastrous. Donald Gorm, the Macdonald chief, agreed to an arranged marriage with Rory Mor's sister despite never having met her. Unfortunately, she only had one eye, so Donald Gorm sent her back to Dunvegan mounted on a one-eyed horse, with a one-eyed groom, followed by a one-eyed dog. Needless to say, war ensued. The King frequently attempted to put a stop to the hostilities but when they did eventually cease, it seemed more due to exhaustion on both sides than mediation.

Rory Mor mellowed with age and in 1609 even consented to abide by the Statutes of Iona. These gave the King overall authority in the Isles and so curtailed the power of the Highland Chiefs. Rory was bound over to keep the peace and even had the amount of wine his household was allowed limited to ten litres a day! Rory behaved so well that lands that had been confiscated were returned to him. Indeed his relations with the King improved so markedly that in 1613 he was knighted at Greenwich and the King invited him to visit London whenever he wished.

In 1623 he was made a burgher of the City of Edinburgh and a Justice of the Peace and it was then that he decided to make the castle more comfortable by constructing the east wing.

After Rory Mor's death in 1626, the relationship between the MacLeods and royalty continued to be harmonious. They proved themselves to be staunch Royalists by fighting for Charles II at Worcester in 1651, where 700 clansmen were killed. This great loss of life led to the other Highland Chiefs deciding that the MacLeods should not send men to fight until they had built up their strength once more. Thus the clan did not take an active part in either the 1715 or 1745 Risings, which saved them from the forfeiture of land which would have inevitably ensued. The MacLeods did not remain totally uninvolved however, as they frequently harboured Royalist refugees. Flora Macdonald, whose daughter was married to the Tutor of MacLeod, stayed at Dunvegan and many of Bonnie Prince Charlie's relics are there, including the broken Amen glass given to Donald MacLeod of Galtrigall, who brought the Prince over the sea to Skye.

Some improvements were made to the castle by Iain Breac, the eighteenth chief and Rory Mor's grandson: but the major remodelling was carried out by General Norman MacLeod in the last decade of the

eighteenth century. He re-roofed the old tower and converted the old banqueting hall into a comfortable Georgian drawing room. In 1810 the entrance hall was added, as well as another storey to the south wing.

By the mid-nineteenth century the MacLeods found themselves badly in debt. But Norman, who became the twenty-fifth chief in 1835, never shirked his duties as clan chief and on one occasion raised the funds to feed 8000 of his more destitute clansmen. In 1840 he added two more storeys with battlements to Rory Mor's range and a porch to the entrance hall. However the disastrous potato famine of 1847–51 finally bankrupted the family and for a number of years economic necessity obliged them to let Dunvegan.

Today the castle is inhabited by John MacLeod of MacLeod, the twenty-ninth chief. He continues the work of his grandmother, Dame Flora MacLeod, who had formed the clan society and so rekindled the spirit of the MacLeods. John MacLeod plays an active role in the affairs of the Clan Parliament but, for him, his prime responsibility is to maintain the castle as his actual home and as the spiritual home of the MacLeod name.

·𝓕OULIS·

FOULIS CASTLE (*left*). *Foulis has seen many changes over the past 800 years, not least in 1745, when it had to be rebuilt after being destroyed by the Jacobites. At that time the main coaching road used to run past the front door, under the tower, which led to more peaceful travellers stopping to demand bread and water or, if the weather was particularly vile, shelter for the night. The Lairds of Foulis became increasingly irritated by this stream of visitors and so resited the road to its present position along the bottom of the park by the sea. The courtyard pictured here used to house the carriages and horses and had a laundry and carpenter's to one side and a bothy for coachmen and estate workers on the other. Recently Captain Patrick Munro and his wife have turned the courtyard into a flower garden and their excavations have brought to light many old features such as the cobbles.*

THE FIRST DESIGNATED BARON of Foulis was Hugh Munro, who died in 1126, and it was later in that century, 1164, that Donald Munro is reputed to have built the original tower of Foulis Castle. At this time the Munros owed fealty to the Earls of Ross, and so it was only in 1476, when the latter forfeited their estates, that the Munros held the land direct from the Crown. Even then this was subject to the rather quixotic proviso of the payment of a bucket of snow on Midsummer's Day to cool the King's wine if demanded.

Throughout their history the Munros have been soldiers by nature and records show that they fought bravely at Bannockburn in 1314, Halidon Hill in 1333 and Pinkie in 1547. When no major battles were taking place they amused themselves with local skirmishes against neighbouring clans. One such clash was with the Mackenzies in 1542 and it has always been referred to as 'The Pass of the Shoes', on account of the Munros' habit of tying their brogues to their chests to afford them better protection.

In many ways the attitude of the Munros towards fighting was similar to that of the mercenaries of today. When Sir Robert Munro found himself forced to mortgage the estate in 1619, having wasted away a fortune through profligate living, he raised a regiment of Munros to serve in the Thirty Years War in an attempt to pay off his debts. Then, in 1629, he offered his services to King Gustavus Adolphus of Sweden and was appointed colonel of a cavalry regiment at Leipzig.

As in the 1715 Rising the Munros supported the Government in 1745 and had Foulis set on fire by the Jacobites for their pains. Luckily they received a grant of £5000 from the Government as a reward for their loyalty which enabled the castle to be rebuilt by 1754. Although now free from any threat from the Jacobites the Munros soon managed to create problems of their own making. Sir Hugh Munro, the eighth Baronet, had as his only offspring a daughter, Mary Seymour, who was born out of wedlock (although he later married her mother). His cousin, Charles

THE OLD KITCHEN *(right). This was still in daily use until 1948. It was presumably a healthy place to work as one of the servants, Katherine Mackenzie, who lived to the age of 117, worked at Foulis for 103 years, and could still walk a mile a day until a few days before she died.*

INSIDE THE TOWER *(right). This is one of the three fortified towers which can be found in the courtyard. Each contained four inverted-keyhole gun loops, facing north, south, east and west, which date from the early sixteenth century. Designed with defence as the paramount concern, each has five-foot-thick walls and a vaulted ceiling three foot thick in the centre and four and a half foot thick at the sides. The living quarters were situated above it.*

Munro of Culrain, realized that if he could prove Mary's illegitimacy he stood to inherit both the title and Foulis Castle itself. There then followed protracted litigation and a fortune was spent by both families in legal costs. As if this were not enough, Sir Hugh was so determined to stop anything from falling into his cousin's hands that he ordered the sale of all the furniture in the castle by auction, leaving extra instructions that anything not sold was to be burnt.

Ironically, although Sir Hugh eventually won the case, his daughter died a mere nine months after his own death, and so what was left of the inheritance duly passed to Charles Munro after all.

Since then Munros have been blessed with a rather quieter existence and the castle has been gradually repaired and renovated. Much of the work has been done by Captain Patrick Munro of Foulis, the present chief of Clan Munro, and his wife, with the help of the Historic Buildings Council. Captain Munro takes his clan responsibilities very seriously and loves welcoming visiting clan members.